The Cosmic Egg Timer

Introducing Astrological Psychology

by
Joyce Hopewell
and
Richard Llewellyn

HopeWell
Knutsford, England

First published in the U.K. in 2004 by HopeWell.

Second revised 2011 edition was reworked and improved
and did not include the cartoons from the original.

This third edition further revised 2018, with illustrations newly in colour.

HopeWell
130 Grove Park, Knutsford
Cheshire WA16 8QD, U.K.

Edited by Barry Hopewell.

Cover image courtesy of agsandrew and Shutterstock.

ISBN 978-0-9956736-2-5

Dedicated to

Bruno and Louise Huber, pioneers of this wonderful new synthesis of astrology and modern growth psychology.

About the Authors

Richard Llewellyn began studying astrology with the Mayo School, gaining their Diploma in 1981. On discovering the work of Bruno and Louise Huber at their Astrological Psychology Institute (API) in Zurich, he became inspired by their psychological approach to astrology, soon gaining the API Diploma. Supported by the Hubers Richard co-founded the UK-based correspondence school API(UK) in 1983, served as *principal* and then *principal emeritus* for many years. He also completed a three year professional training with the Psychosynthesis & Education Trust.

Joyce Hopewell's early career was as a teacher and social worker. After being awarded her API Diploma in 1987 she took over as *principal* of API(UK) in 1991, and has been *principal emeritus* of the newly formed Astrological Psychology Association since 2006. Joyce has a Diploma in Personal Psychosynthesis, has featured in a popular monthly astrological psychology programme on local radio, and produced a regular blog on astrological psychology.

Both Richard and Joyce have extensive experience of astrological counselling, course tutoring and facilitation of experiential workshops in astrological psychology and psychosynthesis. Each has spoken at international astrology conferences.

Contents

1. Introduction

"The basic concept of astrological psychology is based on the understanding of man as a whole; he has a psyche which is linked with the environment, but he is also a spiritual entity who can be responsible for itself."
Bruno and Louise Huber, API code of ethics

There is today an increasing desire of people to understand and develop themselves, and find their own true role in assisting humankind to find a just and sustainable way of living on the Earth. There are many paths towards this goal, including various religions, philosophies and psychologies. This book focuses on one of these – astrological psychology.

Since ancient times astrology has helped people to understand themselves and their place in the universe. The twentieth century saw the development of the modern science of psychology. As this unfoldment proceeded, there came an increasing awareness that astrology and psychology can offer complementary insights into the development of the human being.

Pioneers in investigating this convergence were the Swiss astrologers and psychologists Bruno and Louise Huber, who developed their own simplified psychological approach to astrology after years of research in collaboration with Roberto Assagioli, founder of the growth psychology known as psychosynthesis.

The method developed by the Hubers both cut down and extended traditional approaches to astrology. The most important and best correlated features of astrology were included, and less important features omitted. Radical new approaches were incorporated – notably the use of colour and intuitive images in the birth chart, the psychological meaning of patterns of aspects, recognition of cycles of energy in the astrological houses, the Family Model which enables understanding of key childhood influences, and the Life Clock which highlights influences at work at different times of life.

The result is a powerful tool, both for self-understanding and for helping others in their own lives. Detailed exploration of the Huber approach invariably changes the lives of those so engaged, and enables them to touch the lives of others.

The Hubers' teachings were initially presented in the German language. They founded the Astrological Psychology Institute (API) at Zurich in 1968, offering courses leading to a professional Diploma qualification.

After studying extensively with the Hubers, Richard Llewellyn and Pam Tyler founded an English-language correspondence school of astrological counselling in 1983. Since then over a thousand students from across the world have passed through this school, originally API(UK) and then the Astrological Psychology Association. Joyce Hopewell was for many years its Principal and is now Principal Emeritus.

As well as being prime source material for those learning astrological psychology, we hope that this work will be of interest to the general reader seeking more insight into themselves and their own growth process. It should be of particular interest to astrologers and psychologists/ counsellors who are not familiar with the Huber approach, but wish to gain an insight into it.

Making effective use of this book

You are likely to gain much more from this book if you read it in conjunction with looking at your own birth chart, drawn in the Huber style. If you do this, you will not only better understand the material presented, but also find out more about your own inner self – who you are, where you have come from, where you are going and what might be the blockages to your own growth.

You could also look at the charts of one or two family or friends, perhaps gaining some insight into what makes them tick. But beware that the chart does not dictate what you are; it shows potential that may or may not be realised in any particular human being.

We hope that this taste of what can be unveiled and achieved will whet your appetite to further your study and practice of this exciting approach to astrological psychology. Be aware that you will need to study the subject in greater depth before you can consider using this approach in a practical counselling situation. For resources to help your further study, see the website www.astrologicalpsychology.org.

2. Astrological Psychology in Context

"Astrology must be reborn and must perform again for our modern world, made chaotic by an unbridled and false individualism and by the sudden opening of psychological dams, the task of practical integration that has always been its own."

Dane Rudhyar, *The Astrology of the Personality* 1936

Historical Context

Occasionally on a clear night, even in the modern world, you might happen on a dark place, miles from any bright lights. Standing there, are you not awe-struck by the wonder of the heavens? Surely there is meaning, as well as beauty, here.

In these days of electric lighting it is easy to forget just how important the stars and planets were for our ancestors. The heavens were naturally the subject of observation and speculation, and correlations were often noticed between events on earth and configurations of the heavens.

It seems likely that the Sumerians established the basis of modern astrology around 6000BC. Since then astrological ideas have gone through periods of popularity, and through periods of neglect and denial.

A notable flowering came in the ancient Greek era; in 560 BC Asklepius established at Kos the first of many temples based on three prime disciplines – astrology, mythology and interpretation of dreams. Astrology was then a prime tool for understanding the human psyche.

In the second century AD Ptolemy established a synthesis of Hellenistic astrology/ astronomy that has been influential to this day.

After the so-called Dark Ages, the 15th century European Renaissance was fired by the rediscovery of Greek ideas, leading to the religious Reformation and the rise of modern science. Astrologers such as Johannes Kepler and Marcilio Ficino were prime movers in this process, as was the alchemist Isaac Newton.

This rise of science has led to the technological wonders of the modern world. However, with the coming of the so-called Enlightenment, the new scientific emphasis on objectivity, reductionism and materialism soon began to dominate public discourse in the West, generally disparaging astrology and even spirituality.

The last century has seen the culmination of a number of trends which apparently threaten the future of humanity itself – massively rising world population, an aggressive capitalism founded on the oil-based economy, leading to environmental degradation and massive species loss, destruction of indigenous communities and their way of life, not to mention ever-more-destructive and inhumane methods of warfare.

Humanity is in crisis. Our civilisation, as many in history, is threatened with various disasters largely of its own making. What can be done to address such a crisis, and how can astrology, often denigrated through the ages by both religion and science, help?

Psychology and Spirituality

Just as the 20th century began to see the worst fruits of materialism, it also saw the green shoots of a new and sustainable way of looking at things. With the creation of the science of psychology in the early 1900s, notably through the work of Sigmund Freud, we began to understand what makes human beings tick.

Carl Jung's psychology moved on and embraced symbolism and dreams, adding the concept of synchronicity – meaningful coincidence. The psychological knowledge of the Greeks was being reclaimed and carried forward.

Increased exposure to Eastern religions was also leading to new ideas of spirituality gaining ground in the West, driven by major figures such as H. P. Blavatsky and Alice Bailey.

Roberto Assagioli began to bring these threads together by establishing the psychology of psychosynthesis, which takes into account the transpersonal or spiritual dimensions of experience. Assagioli developed a model of the personality – the *Egg* – that encapsulates its conscious and unconscious aspects and its link with the divine.

In the middle of the Egg is the conscious personal self, surrounded by its field of conscious self awareness (the

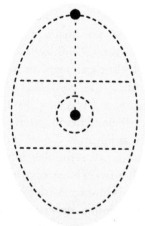

Assagioli's Egg

circle). Other parts of the Egg's interior represent various aspects of the unconscious. At the top is the Higher Self, the link with the divine/ spiritual nature.

Assagioli saw how the individual generally acts inconsistently, being at different times one of a number of independent subpersonalities that have evolved to cope with life's different circumstances. What is needed is a process of synthesis and development of the will, to bring coherence to this scattered personality. With such synthesis we can effectively approach our spiritual essence.

The resurgence of spirituality continues to gain ground in the West. The dominant consumerist materialism inevitably does not in the end prove satisfying. Many people want more in their lives, but do not necessarily see value in the declining religions and their churches, notably because of some of their disreputable history (e.g. the Inquisition).

There is a consensus of great minds, well documented by Huston Smith, that there is in fact a common golden thread at the heart of all the world's religions, providing a spiritual goal for each individual. To find their path to that goal, some people find the framework of organised religion helpful; to others it is at best unnecessary, or even superficial and hypocritical.

It is clear from even a superficial understanding of spiritual values, such as the golden rule of 'do as you would be done by', that a more spiritual humanity will be a kinder humanity, with each person more in tune with themselves, with their fellows, and with the natural world. It does not seem unreasonable to suggest that only by becoming more spiritual will humanity gain the wisdom to solve the problems of the deteriorating global environment, caused as it is by individual human decisions and their life styles.

Changing Paradigm

As well as increased questioning of materialism, a new paradigm of science is emerging, driven by the evolution of science itself, notably the insights of Quantum Theory and Relativity. The difference in viewpoint is profound, and can be expected to increasingly pervade the general discourse of ideas. We will only consider two aspects of this change – objectivity and reductionism.

Quantum phenomena cannot be observed entirely objectively. The result of an experiment depends on what you were looking for. Is matter composed of elementary particles or of waves of energy? Look for waves and you find waves; look for particles and that is what you find.

So science is having to recognise the subjective and the inevitable role it plays in experiment. The consciousness of the scientist cannot be neglected, and there is an increase in the attempts of scientists and philosophers to understand the nature of consciousness itself, which of course cannot be explained in materialistic terms.

Quantum phenomena also show that physically disconnected objects are mysteriously linked together. The universe is more interconnected and wholistic than is allowed for in the reductionist model of inanimate, independent parts.

There is a corresponding increasing scientific interest in interconnected systems and organic wholes. Many environmental problems come about because people tinker with parts of a system without understanding the whole system – for example, a tiny marine organism *Emiliana Huxleyi* is a key to global rainfall. And an organic whole is more than its parts – a hive of bees is more effective than the sum of its individuals.

In the 1930s Dane Rudhyar gave us the complementary insight that, just as mathematics is the symbolic language for understanding objective science, so astrology is the symbolic language for understanding organic wholes. Each whole is born, lives a life cycle and dies – and the astrological configuration of the universe at birth gives us information shaping that life cycle. Rudhyar used this insight in promoting a psychological approach to astrology.

The Hubers and Astrological Psychology

Bruno and Louise Huber refined this marriage of astrology with psychology into a practical and effective methodology.

In the early 1950s this young Swiss couple were called to Geneva to help form a branch of the Arcane School – a spiritual school providing courses of study and meditation based around the works of Alice Bailey. This early spiritual grounding provided the rock of dedication to the well-being of others that underpinned all their subsequent work.

Bruno and Louise were then inspired to work with Assagioli in Florence for three years, helping with his development of the new psychosynthesis. During this time they used Assagioli's psychological research data to test and extend their astrological knowledge. They confirmed for themselves many facets of traditional astrology, and discovered new insights such as the Life Clock and the Dynamic Energy Curve.

Determined to put this knowledge to use for the benefit of humanity, the Hubers devoted their lives to developing this blend of astrology and psychology – consulting, researching and teaching at their Astrological Psychology Institute in Zürich.

They took what they found to be the best of traditional astrology, and linked it with Assagioli's psychosynthesis. Their method involves the innovative use of colour to highlight patterns and meaning in the birth chart, and the use of three separate charts to address different aspects of the person's life.

Example Huber Chart
04.11.2003, 16:39 53°19′N 002°22′W

The Huber Method is now a thriving tradition, which has been taught to tens of thousands of students, through API-related schools teaching in German, English and Spanish. Its aims include helping the personal growth of each student, producing counsellors who can be entrusted with helping the development of a human being using astrology as a tool, producing further teachers to spread the word, and stimulating further research.

Individual Growth and Transformation

As already mentioned, the psychosynthesis model identifies the existence within the individual psyche of a number of subpersonalities.

In the astrological birth chart the planets correspond with basic drives which are striving to come into consciousness, like young plants growing in a garden.

Particular subpersonalities will tend to have formed at times when particular drives were active, so we can perhaps begin to see that there may be an indirect relationship between our subpersonalities and the planetary positions in the birth chart.

When we are born all action is unconscious. Slowly we evolve to become conscious beings. Unfortunately, our subpersonalities often prevent this coming into consciousness, because they have become crystallised as habitual patterns of behaviour and defence mechanisms. Perhaps we always do something because, as a child, something bad once happened to us.

To grow beyond these crystallised patterns of behaviour, we must first recognise and become aware of them. At any particular time in our lives the position of the planets in the astrological birth chart can help us to pin point the drives that are currently striving to come into consciousness, hence giving clues to our psychological state and subpersonalities.

Once we have become aware, we have the possibility of doing something about it. First there must be an acceptance that 'I am indeed like this', then we can begin to understand the pattern and how it is triggered. Of course, the acceptance of negative emotions that may be uncovered, such as fear and anger, is not easy. Copious amounts of love and forgiveness are likely to be required.

Eventually, we can develop choices about how we could change behaviour, ultimately deciding by an act of will what we are going to do to change.

Astrological psychology can help cut to the quick of a psychological problem in short order. Bruno Huber said that in one or two consultations he could reach the same position with the client as with months of traditional psychoanalysis.

We can see this process as one of refinement: removing the blocks to the expression of the essential spiritual qualities that are our true potential. In the Huber method the chart includes indicators of particular significance for this uncovering of our spiritual destiny – for example in the positioning of the Moon's North Node.

So astrological psychology can help to give understanding and meaning to the life and growth process of each person, from the little problems of subpersonalities to their essential spiritual destiny. This is indeed a powerful method for helping our individual process of growth and transformation.

Human and Planetary Transformation

We began this chapter by highlighting the predicament humanity finds itself in, with environmental disaster and other catastrophes imminent. The need is clearly for humanity to collectively change and transform.

Einstein pointed out that problems cannot be solved with the same level of thinking that created them; something more is needed. For humanity, this means transformation to a higher level of being. Let us recognise that humanity is us – you and me and many others. When we change ourselves the world can change; if we do not change the world will not. As Gandhi said: "Be the change you want to see in the world."

We can also consider the Egg model as applying to humanity as a whole. The *mass personality* at the centre of this Egg is on that same journey of growth and transformation towards the Higher Self/ spiritual.

Humanity's Egg is at the working interface between the top down process of the Universal Self/ Ultimate Reality seeking to come into consciousness in matter, and the bottom up process of evolution of earth from plants to animals to human beings, coming into self consciousness.

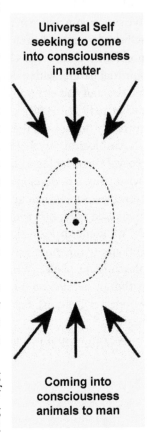

Universal Self seeking to come into consciousness in matter

Coming into consciousness animals to man

Evolution of Humanity

Perhaps this begins to define a purpose for astrology because it gives a sense of the larger plan. Not only a reason for us being here but also for doing something with our lives. Something which helps with the manifestation of transpersonal qualities in matter and therefore with the evolution of humanity.

These transpersonal qualities such as joy, beauty, peace, wisdom, which originate from the source of everything, are looking for form in which to manifest. And we are that form.

We can see that our own personal use of astrological psychology is participating in this grand evolution of humanity.

Conclusion

We can choose to live in a blind materialistic world, driven by essentially selfish desires and attachments, and continue to exacerbate today's problems. Or we can choose to become awakened to our own true spiritual nature, with a dominant empathy and compassion with all our fellows and the creation. With the latter we would hardly collectively put at peril the ability of our planet to support human life, as we are currently doing with the former.

Astrological psychology provides a path through which we can recover the meaning in our own lives. In that process we transform our personality and develop our spirituality. We grow and contribute more effectively to the great growth of humanity, learning to live in a glorious revitalised symbiosis with our Earth.

We come to learn that we are spiritual beings, here for a purpose. Perhaps at this time we have come to earth to help with the business of saving the planet. Without our joint efforts it will surely temporarily withdraw permission for billions of humans to dominate and ravage its wonderful creations. Let us go about this work with a will, and in good heart.

We can be so much more than we are today…

Summary – Astrological Psychology in Context

- Astrological ideas have always gone through periods of popularity, then neglect and denial.

- The 20th century saw in the West the worst fruits of materialism, leading to potential environmental catastrophe – but also to the rediscovery of psychology and spirituality.

- Modern science is showing that all is interconnected – and wholes are more than the sum of parts. Dane Rudhyar suggested that astrology is the symbolic language for understanding organic wholes, and promoted a psychological approach to astrology.

- Roberto Assagioli developed his psychology of psychosynthesis, taking into account the transpersonal/ spiritual.

- Bruno and Louise Huber worked with Assagioli and used his research to test and extend their understanding of astrology. They confirmed parts of existing astrology and discovered new insights. The Hubers developed their own simplified Method and established the Astrological Psychology Institute in Zürich. Their approach is now a thriving tradition.

- Astrological psychology can help the individual's psychological and spiritual growth process, and facilitate the counselling process. It can provide a fast track to uncovering psychological problems.

- The raising of human consciousness necessary to address today's problems is supported by astrological psychology through its enabling of the raising of individual consciousness.

3. The Five Levels of Human Existence

"The centre has many names. Some call it soul, psyche, anima or atman; others call it spirit, higher self or monad. In Indian philosophy, the life-giving centre of man is called the divine spark or fohat. In the Greek and Christian cultures we associate it with entelechy. In reality, we cannot describe and understand this essential core in satisfactory terms. That is why we leave this circle in the middle open and do not draw aspects through it."

Bruno & Louise Huber, *The Astrological Houses*

Astrological psychology is human centred. It is less concerned with external events and what might be going to happen to us, and is more interested in focussing on what is taking place at a deeper, inner motivational level. It seeks to understand the human being's psychological responses and reactions to the environment and the outside world. With this in mind, the approach to interpreting the birth chart outlined in this book is to first of all explore what is going on inside rather than begin by looking at what might be coming at us from the outside.

We start any interpretative work at the centre of the chart, where there is an empty circle in Huber-style charts. We work from this space, moving from the inside of the chart outwards, rather than trying to find a way into the chart from the outside. The chart is composed of five separate levels, the five levels of human existence. These levels form an essential ground plan and starting point for any interpretation, so it's important to have an understanding of them right from the start.

Let's first take a look at our example Huber chart on page 7.

The Central Core

The circle at the centre of the chart is known as the central core. This is the first, and deepest, of the five levels. This circle is always left clear – no planetary aspects are drawn through it. It symbolizes soul, spirit, and the doorway to universal energy. Some people might experience it as the place where we connect with our Higher Self, or God; some people would say it is where they connect with

Central Core

higher, transpersonal energies. In this space our personal self and the transpersonal Self can meet.

The central core is the place we can move into when we want to feel whole; here we can step into our own centre – symbolized by the circle at the centre – and can connect with something beyond ourselves. It represents the spark of divinity within each and every one of us.

If you were in a room full of people with their birth charts drawn up in this way, everybody's chart would look different. But if the charts were all gathered together and then piled up one on top of the other, they would each have one thing in common: the circle in the centre. We all have this central core, this spark of divinity; it's common to all. And this is where our chart interpretation begins, no matter whose chart is being used. This clear space at the centre of the chart, representing the essential divinity of the person, is always acknowledged first.

The Aspect Level

There is abundant animating energy at the central core – our own centre and the centre of the chart. This energy cannot be contained; it moves outwards and is embodied by the aspects at the next level. The second level of the chart contains the aspect structure, which represents our unconscious motivation. This is where we look to see the unconscious driving forces of the individual. The aspects are pulsating with energy of different kinds and qualities, and the aspect structure

The Aspect Level

offers valuable information about what makes us tick, what really drives us.

The motivation shown here is largely unconscious, but we can get to know and understand it better – and we can choose to work on familiarizing ourselves with what truly makes us tick. Anything that is unconscious, such as our inner motivation, can be brought into consciousness. We can recognise it, we can accept it and we can begin to work with it. Then we can start to transform it, change it, integrate it, and allow it to become an integrated part of our lives. Such integration and development of the whole person is the aim of the approach to psychology known as psychosynthesis.

Although the motivation shown in this part of the chart might start off by being unconscious, we can thus bring it into greater awareness so that we can move forward feeling more firmly in the driving seat of our lives.

Level of the Planets

At the third level the planets represent our psychological drives. We each have a variety of drives – for example, the drive to communicate, the drive to be safe and secure, to be loved, to assert ourselves, to form relationships. The planets positioned at this level provide an energy path from the central core and aspect structure to the environment, or outside world.

Level of the Planets

The aspects energise the planets by transmitting energy to them from the central core, lighting them up like light bulbs. But how they are able to shine and glow will depend on the quality of energy that the aspects transmit to them. The planets also have to react and respond to the demands coming at them from the outside world, and they do this through the qualities of the sign and house they are placed in

To summarise so far, the planets respond and react to the energy transmitted to them from the central core, via the aspect structure, and they also respond and react to the demands of the outside world.

Level of the Signs of the Zodiac

At the fourth level we have the signs of the zodiac. These represent our inherited traits and qualities, the characteristics that have been passed down through generations of humankind. These traits are not just inherited via the immediate preceding generation, but come from a long line of ancestors, reaching back across the centuries. The archetypal qualities of the signs are our human inheritance (Chapter 7).

Level of the Signs

They and their characteristics can be viewed as the costumes that are donned by the planets, each sign having a different costume according to its qualities. Taking this analogy further, we can see that the energy of the planets will be modified in some way if they assume the costume of the sign in which they are placed.

Level of the Houses

The fifth and final level of the chart is where we find the houses. These represent the environment, the world around us. Each house cusp is marked around the outside edge of the chart. In some conventional charts, the houses are scored into the chart wheel, but here each of the five levels is discrete. This is deliberate, symbolic and significant. Each level of the chart is separate, and represents a different field of human existence. Therefore we don't mix up one level with another; each represents a different part of the whole person in this model of human existence.

Level of the Houses

The houses are on the outside of the chart because this is where all the levels come into contact with the environment. The houses represent the world around us, our world, where we live and express the energies and potentials available to us, that are shown in the chart.

An Alternative Description

We have described how, using the five levels of the chart as a guide in chart interpretation, we can move from the inside of the chart outwards towards our environment and the world in which we live, expressing, making manifest and grounding our own unique energy pattern through the houses, which represent our world and environment.

We now take an alternative and complementary look at the five levels of human existence. Consider the idea that universal energy is seeking to become manifest, to express itself in the world of form and matter, in which we human beings live and of which we are a part. As this divine energy seeks expression through us in the world of form and matter, so form and matter (that's us too) which have evolved to a certain level of consciousness seek to return to the spirit or the divine source.

Chapter 2 already introduced the ideas of individual growth and transformation, which can be seen as part of this process of raising consciousness and return to the source.

The following diagram relates these ideas, of spirit seeking expression through matter and matter seeking reconnection with spirit, with the five levels of the chart. The chart is shown as a triangular cone, as if pulled upwards so that the central core is at the top, and all five levels are intact.

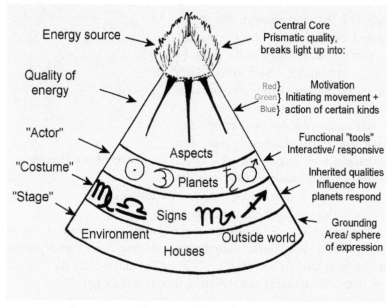

Expression of Energy through the Five Levels

The circle at the centre acts as the doorway to universal energies, becoming the top of the cone, open and forever receptive to this. In the diagram we can see the effect of energy moving through the aspect structure via the planets, signs and houses as it seeks expression in the material world through the personality.

The central core of the chart – open to this energy source – is like a pure white light which contains the aspect colours of red, green and blue. As if through a prism, the energy is broken up into these three colours which are the colours of the aspects used in Huber-style charts. Each colour represents a different quality, which is filtered through into the next level of the chart and shown in the aspects. The aspect level of the chart is where we look for inner motivation. The balance of the aspect colours will indicate predispositions to act and respond in different ways. This level is concerned with the quality of the energy.

The energy, still seeking grounding and expression is then relayed to the planets, representing our drives and the psychological tools with which we respond to the world and interact with our environment. Some of our planets may be more consciously awake than others, more developed. They are sensitive, receptive and fizzing with the energy they receive from the centre of the chart; at the same time they are called upon to respond to the demands of the environment, which may require more (or less) of how they are seeking to express this.

As already described, the planets can be the *actors*, or different sub-personalities, through which we express this energy. The signs are the inherited/ passed on from generation to generation *costumes* that they wear, which will modify the planets' actions, expression and movement. The houses are the *stage* upon which they perform and seek expression in the world; the positions of the planets within the houses give us further clues as to whether they will perform from the wings or from centre stage front.

Conclusion

We began at the centre of the chart. Pure energy is pulsing forth from this point and is picked up by and filtered through the aspects, which show us the various qualities of the energy they are carrying.

The energy, seeking grounding in the outside world, is relayed to the planets which represent our psychological drives.

The houses are vitally important because they are the areas of expression and manifestation for the energy coming from the centre of the chart, and that energy can be seen as divine potential which seeks expression through us in our lives.

The houses show us where in our world we can best express this energy, be a creator, contribute to our own well-being and that of others, and be, in the fullest sense of the word, a pioneer. And it is here, in the environment, the world around us, that we can reconnect with spirit in matter, through our relationship with the earth and our relationships with the people around us.

Summary – The Five Levels of the Chart

- There are five distinct and independent levels of a chart:

  The circle at the centre, the central core, represents the essential spiritual self

  The aspect structure represents unconscious motivation

  The planets represent psychological drives

  The signs represent inherited characteristics, which colour those drives

  The houses represent the environment, the world around.

- Energy from the centre seeks grounding in the environment; spirit seeks grounding in matter. From the centre of the chart, energy flows out. It is filtered through the aspects and relayed to the planets, coloured by the signs, and then expressed through the houses – the environment.

4. Looking at the Whole Chart

"Viewed in its entirety the aspect structure is a symbolic representation of our consciousness, formed by the life energies available to us. That's why it is possible to 'see' the inner motivation inherent in a chart only by means of our senses, by means of a meditative approach."

Bruno Huber, *Astrological Psychosynthesis*

Orientation – the Angles

It will be useful to those unfamiliar with astrology if we first introduce four basic reference points in the chart – the AC, DC, MC and IC, shown on our example chart. These are part of the house system (Chapter 8).

AC, DC, MC, IC
Four Basic Reference Points

If you imagine a notional line between the *ascendant* (AC) and the *descendant* (DC) opposite, this line represents the actual east-west horizon on earth at the time and place of birth. This is shown to be approximately horizontal in computer-generated charts.

A second dimension is provided by the *midheaven* (MC), representing the highest position of the Sun on the day of birth, and the lower heaven or *imum coeli* (IC) opposite.

The notional line between MC and IC provides a vertical dimension to the chart. In most charts, this line is not actually at right angles to the AC/DC line, the angle being dependent on the longitude of the birth, place and the time of year. These two notional lines are called the *angles* of the chart.

Chart Image

One of the most important things we can do when starting to look at a chart is to do simply that – to look. Setting aside and perhaps even temporarily forgetting any astrology you already know, the first way into the chart is via the senses, the eyes and the intuition.

Cast your mind back to the time when you were a small child. Maybe you had a coal fire or wood burner in the house where you grew up. Can you remember looking into the embers of the fire and seeing pictures or scenes, faces or figures? Or you may have looked at clouds in the sky: "That one looks like a dog... now it's changed and looks more like a dragon," and so on. Using your eyes, senses and imagination, you were perhaps able to see pictures and images, based on the shapes you saw in the clouds or the fire.

Similarly when first looking at a chart, we can train ourselves to look for an intuitive picture or image emerging from the energy patterns reflected in the chart. We do this by looking at the overall aspect structure in the large central area of the chart. In the context of astrological psychology, this area relates to the unconscious motivation of a person.

Often the essence of the person is contained within this area of the chart. Through developing the intuition we can gain a sense of the person simply by looking at this central area of the chart, and absorbing and reflecting upon the pictures or images that we see there.

You can try this out for yourself using a Huber-style chart. Allow yourself to get a sense of what is in the chart. From this a picture or image may emerge. Images people have seen in charts are as diverse as a flower opening, a tent or marquee, a pyramid, a butterfly, a space rocket, an open book, a yacht, a flag – the variety is limitless, based upon what has been intuitively seen and perceived from the chart.

You may not see an image or picture, but may instead have a strong sense of a predominant colour in the aspect structure, or a sense that everything in the chart is spread out, or squashed, or clinging to one particular area of the chart. So, if you are unable to see an image or picture, be aware of whether you are picking up something in the chart via your other senses.

The Huber approach emphasises the importance of taking the time to look at a chart before setting off into the realms of deeper and more analytical interpretation. This approach is Jupiterian – using our eyes and our intuition, we look at the chart, taking in the whole picture before moving on to the finer points and details.

This differs from a more conventional Mercurial approach to astrological chart interpretation, where facts and detailed information about the chart are considered first and foremost, using the logical mind – and the overall picture of the chart is not necessarily considered.

Looking at and absorbing the chart in this way is the first foundation stone enabling us to find a way into the natal chart. Chart interpretation can be daunting and difficult, especially if there are a lot of detailed factors to hold in mind at the same time. Using this Jupiterian approach, engaging the senses and the intuition first, we can begin our exploration of any natal chart in considerable depth, by looking at the very essence and the unconscious motivating energies of the person concerned.

Of course, once we have started to look at our own chart in this way, we begin to develop an awareness and understanding of our own motivation which operates at a deep and often unconscious level. And if we work in this way, we also start to bring into consciousness that which was previously largely unconscious.

Note that there are no right or wrong chart images. Two people may see entirely different images in the same chart, each of which gives meaningful insight into the motivation of the subject.

An Example – Birds' Beaks and Megaphones

The chart below has a delicate, tentative feel, although the image(s) we might speculate on are clear and easy to see. There is a flower, trumpet-shaped like a daffodil which is growing from the Sun near the AC (left

Example Chart
22.07.1957 07:00 Much Wenlock, England

hand side) towards the DC (right hand) side of the chart. Or maybe, if we look at this in reverse, it is an aeroplane with delta wings, flying towards the Sun.

The woman whose chart this is says, "Looking at my chart the first image I see is of a bird poking its large beak curiously through that small triangle towards the Sun on the AC (left) side of the chart. This beak seems to be prodding at my Sun, encouraging it to come out.

Another strong image is of three megaphones, or perhaps they are three ear trumpets, coming from the AC (left) to the DC (right) side of the chart. Part of me, perhaps, wants to be noticed and heard (the megaphones), whilst another part prefers to stay in the background taking in as much as I can – the ear trumpets."

We encourage you to practice by looking in this way at other charts, including those published in this book.

Note

When you have found a picture or image in a chart, keep hold of it. It is an invaluable key – or set of keys if there is more than one image – to the chart. Don't throw it away. The chart image can yield up important and relevant information about the person and their unconscious motivation, so it is something to hold in mind and refer to throughout the interpretation of the chart.

Colour and Motivation

When we look at a Huber style chart, often the first impact is of colour – of the aspects and the zodiac signs. Aspect lines are shown in red, blue and green, depending upon their type and nature. The area in the chart allowed for the aspects is large and the eye is immediately drawn towards this. This area of the chart is important as it gives us invaluable information about unconscious motivation and energy – the key to what makes us tick.

The colours red, blue and green corresponds with the three qualities cardinal, fixed and mutable.

Red – Cardinal

A good way to build up an understanding of this colour is to list as many associations as you can for the word *red*. Some examples might be: energy, hot, blood, exciting, vibrant, passion, anger, danger and so on. It is more than likely that you will come up with a list of words which are *action-oriented*.

Now imagine that you can apply these red qualities that you have identified to observable human behaviour. What would a red person be like? How would they go through their daily life? What kind of interests or hobbies would they have? How might their house be arranged and furnished?

Taking this a step further, it is not too difficult to begin to imagine a person who lives life in a red way, full of action and energy and always having something to *do* or initiate. Such a person might have a lot of red aspects in their chart. In the context of astrological psychology, red aspects have a *cardinal*, initiatory, go-ahead quality.

Blue – Fixed

Again, you can start to gain an understanding of the qualities of this colour by listing your associations for the word *blue*. Some suggestions are: serene, calm, resting, security, passive, relaxed, peaceful, spiritual etc. In contrast to activity-oriented red, the list of words you are likely to come up with for blue will be more *passive* in nature.

Now imagine that you can apply the blue qualities that you have identified to observable human behaviour. Consider what a blue person would be like. How would they go through their daily life? What kind of interests or hobbies would they have? And how might their house be arranged and furnished?

A person who lives life in a blue way seeks substance, security, serenity, and stillness, and they would be concerned with the very act of *being*, to enable them to experience and enjoy life. Such a person might have a lot of blue aspects in their chart. Blue aspects have a *fixed* quality, seeking security and stability.

Green – Mutable

As before, listing associations for the word *green* is a good way to start understanding it better. Some such associations might be: changeable, information-seeking, undecided, growth, learning, searching, and questioning. Unlike activity-oriented red and passive, security-seeking blue, the list of words you might come up with for green are focussed more on *growth, sensitivity and awareness.*

Now imagine that you can apply the green qualities that you have identified to observable human behaviour. Consider what a green person would be like. How would they go through their daily life? What kind of interests or hobbies would they have? And how might their house be arranged and furnished?

A person who lives life in a green way will be full of curiosity. They will be sensitive, constantly searching, questing and seeking to understand as much as possible. Their prime motivation would be to *learn*. Such a person might have a lot of green aspects in their chart. In the context of astrological psychology, green aspects have a *mutable*, flexible and changeable quality.

Colour Balance

Having looked at the qualities associated with each of the three aspect colours, we then need to consider how many of each are present in the chart. It is desirable to have all three colours present, as this suggests a rounded representation of all three types of motivation discussed – cardinal (red), fixed (blue) and mutable (green).

We look for a balance of these colours being present in the chart in a ratio of 2 green to 4 red to 6 blue aspects. This *ideal* ratio gives a comfortable balance of awareness and sensitivity (green), action and *doing* energy (red), and appreciation of substance together with stability (blue).

Of course, most charts do not have this ideal ratio. Some may have only red and blue aspects, indicating that the person will tend to see and live life in a black-and-white way, with no shades of grey in between. With no green aspects there may be a lack of awareness and sensitivity.

Occasionally, a chart will have no, or few, blue aspects indicating that the person concerned may be touchy, prickly and sensitive. With only red and green aspects they will always be sensitively primed for action, but they lack blue *substance* aspects to rest and relax into.

Some charts lack red and have a predominance of blue and green aspects. Such people are likely to have strong imaginative and escapist tendencies – the last thing they will feel motivated towards is taking action so they could be demanding to live with, expecting others to do things for them.

It is possible to gain some idea of how the colour balance in a chart might affect the person's motivation by once again simply looking at the chart and gaining a sense of this through what your eyes tell you, but this should be backed up by counting up the number of aspects of each colour in order to get a clearer and more accurate assessment of the kind of energy available to the person.

Chart Shaping and Motivation

The qualities of cardinal, fixed and mutable pervade much of astrological psychology. Having initially looked at the whole chart to see if a visual image can be discerned, the *overall shaping* of the aspect structure can give additional information about unconscious motivation.

Are there just a lot of disconnected lines, or does the overall structure have predominantly quadrangular shapes, or does it have predominantly triangular shapes? These respectively indicate of cardinal, fixed and mutable motivation, which may reinforce, or may counterbalance, the motivation indicated by the balance of colours.

Cardinal Shaping

With cardinal or linear shaping there are no complete figures, only lines which do not come together to form a three or four sided figure. The unconscious motivation of this person is to be restless, changing direction quickly, always seeking to start something new. They want to be doing, to keep moving from one thing to the next, probably expending a lot of energy along the way. Cardinal energy is initiatory, heralding new beginnings, a fresh start, a confident thrust forward and a moving out into the world.

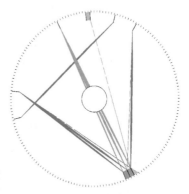

Cardinal Shaping

Fixed Shaping

A chart with fixed shaping has figures of four or more sides. It looks solid and firm, and its overall quadrangular appearance suggests an unconscious motivation towards security and stability. The person needs to know where they stand, to feel safe and secure and to enjoy the substance of life. Fixed energy has an established quality. It seeks to keep things pretty

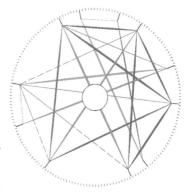

Fixed Shaping

much the same, unchanging, firm and solid. To preserve what is already there is its main purpose.

Mutable Shaping

A chart with mutable shaping is composed of triangular figures which give a feeling of fluidity, suggesting that the person will be able to adapt and adjust quite readily to life circumstances. They will go with the flow, and will not be too upset by change. Mutable energy is moving energy. It adapts and moves on, seeking to keep this momentum of fluidity, shifting, changing but not stopping.

Mutable Shaping

Vertical or Horizontal?

The direction in which the aspect structure of the chart is oriented is another important factor in assessing unconscious motivation.

Vertical Direction

Do the aspects have a vertical appearance? Are they mostly moving from the IC area at the base of the chart towards the MC at the top? If so, the person's motivation will be towards individuality. They will be seeking to stand out in some way, to attain recognition. This might make them ambitious, and they could easily neglect their interpersonal relationships as they focus on their need to be noticed and make their mark in the world.

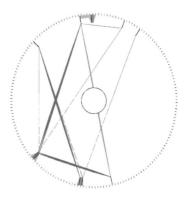

Vertical Direction

Horizontal Direction

Where the aspects move in a more horizontal direction, motivation is more concerned with contact with others. In a horizontal chart the aspects lay predominantly across the chart, from the AC to the DC area. This suggests someone who is oriented towards other people and likely to incorporate this into their personal and professional lives, choosing to work in areas where people skills are important. There is a danger that such people will neglect developing their own individuality in favour of working for and supporting others.

Horizontal Direction

Note that some charts will clearly move in both a vertical and horizontal direction, offering that person possibilities for development in both areas of life and directions.

Summary – Looking at the Whole Chart

- First look for a visual image, using your eyes, senses, intuition.

- The colours red, blue and green correspond with the fundamental qualities cardinal, fixed and mutable respectively:
  red – cardinal – acting
  blue – fixed – being
  green – mutable – learning.

- Look at the colour balance in the chart and see how this relates to motivation and the *ideal* ratio of 2 green: 4 red: 6 blue aspects.

- Look at the overall shaping of the aspect structure and how this relates to motivation:
  cardinal (linear), fixed (quadrangular), mutable (triangular)

- Look at the direction of the aspect structure to see how this relates to motivation:
  vertical (individuality), horizontal (contact)

5. Aspect Patterns

"The aspect structure is a motivational structure. There is the secret of that life in it."

Bruno Huber

In this chapter we explore the meaning of patterns found in the aspect structure around the centre of the chart. When viewed as whole, these recognisable patterns offer immediate relevant information about the potential of the individual – before even considering the planets forming the pattern, and their house and sign position.

The Seven Aspects

First, it is necessary to understand what aspects are, and which of the conventional astrological aspects are central to astrological psychology. There is an aspect between two planets when the angle separating them in the 360 degree circular birth chart is a multiple of 30 degrees (subject to a certain tolerance, known as the orb).

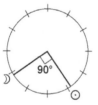

An Angle of 90°

Astrological psychology uses just the seven aspects shown in the diagram. These have been used by astrologers since at least the time of Ptolemy (2nd century AD). Empirical research carried out by Bruno Huber confirmed that they give fundamental insights into the character structure of the individual.

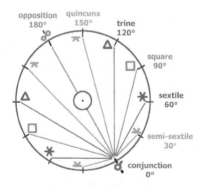

The Seven Aspects

Often in the past, aspects have been pigeon-holed in a somewhat black and white way – particular aspects are said to be good or bad, harmonious or inharmonious. Astrological psychology does not see them in this way, rejecting this approach as psychologically unsound. Rather than regarding aspects as *good* or *bad*, each aspect is seen as having specific qualities full of challenge and opportunity, talent and sensitivity.

The following briefly describes the nature and quality of each aspect, and its associated colour/ motivation (Chapter 4 introduced the meaning of the colours). The corresponding glyphs are as on the above diagram.

Conjunction
The conjunction indicates planets positioned close together. The colour orange is used for this aspect, indicating its close binding nature. The conjunction has the potential to create something new; there may be a seedling talent or ability waiting to be awakened and used. The associated planetary quality is that of the Sun.

Semi-sextile
The semi-sextile is the 30° aspect, shown in green in the natal chart. It is a short aspect with the Mercurial quality of information gathering. The semi-sextile busies itself in short bursts of activity, picking up information and facts from the environment and making small steps in learning.

Sextile
The 60° sextile aspect is associated with the quality of the planet Venus. The nature of this blue aspect is to assimilate and be harmonious. It is adept at making compromises and keeping things on an even keel.

Square
The 90° square aspect is shown in red. The associated planet is Mars, endowing this aspect with active qualities, ensuring that there is an abundance of working energy to be expressed through it.

Trine

The 120° trine is the longer of the two blue aspects. This aspect has a Jupiterian quality, associated with fullness, richness and enjoyment. It has a sensuous, and sometimes indulgent nature.

Quincunx

The 150° aspect is green, implying its searching and gathering qualities. However, with the quincunx the search is a long-term, committed one, reflecting the mentoring and guiding side of Saturn, its associated planet. The quincunx takes big steps in learning.

Opposition

The 180° aspect spans the chart, the longest of the seven aspects. This red aspect has much energy contained within it, but this is blocked and held in a state of tension, awaiting release. The energy may see-saw from one end of the aspect to the other. The associated planetary quality is again Saturn, but in this case the more inflexible side of this planet is seen.

Orbs and One-Way Aspects

For there to be an aspect between two planets the angle between them does not have to be an exact multiple of 30°. There is a tolerance, known as the orb. For example, there is an orb of 4° for a Square aspect between Mars and Saturn – so Mars is Square to Saturn if they lie between 86° and 94° of each other in the chart circle.

For some combinations, the orbs of the two planets are different; one is theoretically *in aspect* while the other is not. Such a *one-way aspect* is shown with a half-dotted line on the side of the planet which is not *in orb*. The relationship between the two planets is in one direction only, so not so strong.

One-way opposition

Summary of meaning of aspects

0° – conjunction – orange – close, binding, new potential

30° – semi–sextile – green – information gathering, perceptive

60° – sextile – blue – seeking harmony, compromises

90° – square – red – active, performance–oriented

120° – trine – blue – enjoyment, bounty, abundance

150° – quincunx – green – questing, searching, committed

180° – opposition – red – tension, suppressed energy

Aspect Patterns

Aspect Patterns were first recognised and developed by Bruno Huber and are based on his empirical research into the charts and real life experiences of the clients and ordinary people whose charts he studied.

In more traditional approaches to astrology it is usual to look at a planet and interpret it in some detail against the zodiac sign in which it is positioned. Less emphasis is placed upon the relationship that the planet has, via aspects, with other planets in the chart.

Astrological psychology is more interested in the interrelationship between the planets, and the recognisable patterns that these connections involve. These patterns are indicators of motivation, so are seen as being of great importance.

There are over forty recognised aspect patterns used in astrological psychology. They relate to motivation coming from the deepest inner level of the chart, the central core – motivation and energies that are often unconscious.

If we can bring these unconscious motivations and resulting behavioural patterns into consciousness, and become more aware of how they operate and manifest in our everyday behaviour, we can start to use them more effectively and productively for ourselves because we will understand how they operate. This awareness and understanding can enrich our lives, help us move beyond our habitual patterns, and understand how we can operate better. We gain better focus and move on, as opposed to getting bogged down and lost upon the way.

General Principles

Building on the description of chart shaping in the last chapter, we can see that the whole chart picture is composed of a number of distinct aspect patterns. Some of these individual patterns are quadrangular in shaping, which corresponds to a fixed motivation. Similarly, triangular shapes correspond with mutable qualities of motivation.

There may also be some disconnected, incomplete lines which do not come together to form either a three or four sided figure. These linear patterns have cardinal motivation.

The colour or colours of the aspect lines present in each individual aspect pattern is also significant; each pattern is made up of one, two or three colours – red, blue and green. Similar guidelines apply to the meaning of these colours as those outlined in the last chapter.

When looking at any aspect pattern it is important to remember that the shape of the pattern will tell us straight away what its overall motivation is, e.g. quadrangular patterns have a fixed motivation, and triangular patterns a mutable motivation. And whereas the shape tells us what its motivation is, the colour of the aspects involved tells us how the pattern will operate and what its mode of action is.

Using these general principles you can begin to understand the motivation behind any aspect pattern.

Note on Planets

It is important to mention here that in all aspect patterns, the expression of the pattern's motivation will be modified and altered by the planets involved. A different set of pinning planets will change the way the pattern is expressed out in the world, but the original meaning and motivation of the pattern remain the same.

An Efficiency Triangle (below) will always be an Efficiency Triangle, but the way it is expressed by different people will be modified by the planets involved in that pattern in their charts.

Common Aspect Patterns

In the following we describe a selection of some of the more common aspect patterns in some detail.

Efficiency Triangle or Achievement Triangle

The Efficiency Triangle is a powerhouse of energy. If you have one in your chart feel fortunate that you are endowed with the ability to perform, act, and have end results to show for it too.

This all-red pattern is made up of two squares and one opposition. It forms a triangle with an obvious apex, and it is the planet positioned at the apex which will be the prime outlet for the energy contained within.

Efficiency Triangle

First, consider the shaping and motivation. The shape is triangular, and triangular shapes have a mutable motivation, giving them fluidity and the ability to be flexible and adaptable – in short, they can move.

Next, consider the colour and motivation of the aspects involved. These are all red, so they endow this pattern with pure cardinal energy. There is plenty of *doing* capacity to be tapped into here. The Efficiency Triangle wants to get on with the job in hand; it seeks to produce and it is capable of doing so with minimum wastage of effort. The colour of this aspect pattern shows us that it will go about this in a cardinal way.

Combine the mutable motivation of this pattern with all that red, cardinal energy and the end result is the potential to be actively involved in taking on a variety of different tasks in a seemingly tireless fashion. The long red aspect – the opposition – acts as a kind of "battery", storing the energy which can then be released along the two shorter red aspects – the squares – and out via the apex at the top of the triangle.

The squares are the real workers in this pattern. Squares need to have something to do, and if they don't have it they become troublesome as the energy gets pent up and seethes quietly beneath the surface, craving release. In more conventional approaches to astrology, squares are often seen as being "problem" aspects, but they will only cause problems if they are not used to their full capacity. In the Efficiency Triangle, they thrive on hard work, utilising the apex planet in this pattern to put this out into the world.

The name Efficiency/Achievement is chosen to be descriptive of its effect. It is also known as a T-Square.

Efficiency Square or Achievement Square

Applying the above guidelines, the Efficiency Square has a fixed motivation as it is quadrangular, and a cardinal mode of action as all its aspects are red — squares and oppositions. Where we find this pattern in someone's chart, its combination of fixed and cardinal qualities gives them the ability to work hard and tirelessly in order to not only feel safe and secure, but to produce something tangible to enhance their security needs. These may often be money, but

Efficiency Square

there may be other, psychological needs that are being fulfilled by their strong drive for hard work.

They may come to identify themselves through their capacity to work. This pattern is frequently found in the charts of self-confessed workaholics, people who can't easily switch off and are always busy doing something, producing something, working to deadlines and generally being indispensable. It is through work that they gain a sense of safety and security.

The Efficiency Square is made up of four square aspects and two oppositions. These red aspects function in a similar way to those in the Efficiency Triangle, but in this pattern there are twice as many of them, meaning that there is potential for twice as much output.

The two oppositions again act as batteries, releasing stored energy through the squares. With four corners to this pattern, the inherent energy will be expressed by the planets positioned there. And if one of these tires, there are three others ready to take over whilst a breather is taken.

This figure was traditionally known as the Grand Cross.

Ambivalence Triangle

People with this frequently occurring pattern often express a huge sense of relief that the behaviour traits associated with it can be recognised in their chart, and that its interpretation and meaning confirms and supports their own real life experience.

The shape is triangular, so its motivation is mutable – flexible, adaptable, changeable.

Ambivalence Triangle

It is composed of both red and blue aspects. Cardinal red aspects are about actively participating – "doing". But blue aspects are fixed by nature, and seek to preserve and maintain; they are much more laid back and are more concerned with simply "being".

So this pattern has a changeable, flexible motivation, but one which is prone to operate in an on (red) and off (blue) way. Hence the ambivalence in its name – and ambivalence is something it has in spades.

People with this pattern find themselves strongly pulled between these two opposing modes of behaviour. On the one hand, they want to get on with the job in hand, and feel they must get down to work and do something. They may castigate themselves about this. At the same time, they are yearning to get away from having to work, and would much rather be in the blue part of the pattern resting, relaxing and playing. When they've had enough of being in work mode, expressing the energy of the red opposition which may pull them this way and that, they will switch over to rest mode and go into the blue part of the pattern, composed of a sextile and a trine aspect.

The planet positioned at the apex where these two blue aspects meet is known as the "escape" planet. Whatever people with this pattern like to do to switch off and relax can often be related to this planet. After being in rest mode for while, tension begins to build again as the person starts to feel the need to be doing something again. Then they will switch back to work and activity mode.

Small Talent Triangle

The Small Talent Triangle is an all-blue figure, made up of two sextile aspects and one trine aspect. Triangular shaping gives it a mutable motivation, fluid and adaptable. The all-blue colour endows it with the fixed qualities described in the previous pattern.

When we see a Talent Triangle in a chart there is an expectation that the person will have

Small Talent Triangle

some latent, underdeveloped ability which they are possibly not putting to full use. The mutable shaping of the pattern might make them flexible, willing to try out new things, but the all-blue nature of the aspects will make progress slow, maybe even static.

The nature of the talent involved in this pattern will be influenced by the planets involved, but it's pretty safe to say that unless the person is aware that the potential for this talent exists, they are unlikely to be tapping into it. The talent inherent in the pattern is likely to be still forming; once it is recognised – and used – by the individual, they can go on to develop and perfect it, whatever its nature.

For example, he may have a natural musical ability, but need to regularly practise the instrument of choice in order to perfect this talent; she may be drawn to acting and the performing arts, yet need to continuously hone and perfect all aspects of stagecraft in order for the talent to blossom fully.

The potential for the kind of talent this figure may encompass is broad. As with all aspect patterns, it is the pinning planets which define its outward expression.

Large Talent Triangle

The related Large Talent Triangle, again all-blue, comprises three trine aspects. Its motivation is similar in nature, but the potential for expressing the talent involved is already developed and in place.

However, people with this pattern often do not bother to use the talent they have been endowed with, so it can be neglected and under-used, or it may simply be lost for lack of attention and expression.

Large Talent Triangle

Kite

The Kite is a large pattern covering a considerable area of the chart and enclosing the central core. Its fixed quadrangular shaping suggests a motivation towards substance and stability. How it will go about achieving this is by applying the blue aspects. But embedded within the pattern is a red opposition forming the main supporting strut of the Kite. If this Kite is ever to fly and get off the ground, this part of the pattern has to be activated. The blue aspects, left to their own devices, will do very little.

Kite

The Kite is often found in the charts of creative people who sometimes find it difficult to produce and manifest their ideas and creativity and bring them into reality. Think of writers who need a strict daily discipline and a place to write that is separate and cut off from the everyday distractions of the world. They also need deadlines, otherwise they are prone to procrastination.

People with Kites may be full of good ideas, with plenty of talent waiting to be used. But without a target or deadline to work towards, the blue aspects beckon, and it is all too easy to put things off for another day. This is when the red *doing* aspect comes into play. The main strut of the Kite, its backbone, has to be activated before the inherent talent and creativity can be released.

It is important to consider the qualities of the planets at the Kite's head and tail. The planet at the tail will tend to hold the Kite back and prevent it from flying, and the planet at the head will indicate where the Kite might head for when it gets off the ground. And it's worth noting which direction the Kite is flying in – is it vertically or horizontally positioned in the chart? This gives additional information on which area of life the talent and creativity of this pattern can be applied to. (See Chapter 8 on the houses.)

Irritation Triangle

This pattern looks like a small green and red dagger. The shape is triangular so its motivation is mutable, and in this case very flexible. It is composed of red and green aspects. Red aspects are the cardinal, *doing*, variety. Green aspects are mutable by nature, associated with awareness and sensitivity. The two green aspects – semi-sextile and quincunx emphasise the overall changeability of this pattern.

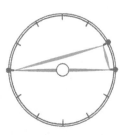

Irritation Triangle

The red opposition aspect holds *doing* energy in a state of tension – until it is released. There is strong mutable motivation at work in the Irritation Triangle, as indicated by both the shaping and the two green aspects. The red-green combination makes for a lot of nervous energy, giving this pattern a fizzy, jumpy quality, hence its name. For irritation you could also read touchy and prickly – people with this pattern tend to be known to fly off the handle.

Behaviour associated with the Irritation Triangle is of a very active kind. People with this pattern in their charts are likely to be those who agree to take on additional tasks to help out. They will more often than not be busy people, and very sensitive as well – sensitive to the needs of others, sensitive that something needs to be done, and flexible in the way they work. So of course they can fit in an extra bit of work to do; yes, and they'll take on that too; and no problem, they'll squeeze that in somewhere, just need to juggle their schedules a bit to make room… and so on.

Then comes the time when they realise they've taken on too much. Something snaps. The pressure is too much. Fuses blow, the person erupts, the green and red dagger comes out in force and people take cover. Then things begin to quieten down; the air is cleared, there are no hard feelings now they've all erupted and been expressed. The person has blown their top, things have calmed down and everything goes back to normal… until, of course, the pressure begins to build up again later on down the line and the same thing happens all over again.

Ear/Eye

This small triangular pattern looks and acts like a tiny radar dish. It is highly sensitive to picking up and storing all manner of information from the surrounding environment. It gathers this in, working most of the time on auto-pilot, stashing it away for future use as and when the occasion demands.

Ear/Eye

Triangular shaping gives a mutable motivation. The Ear/Eye is indeed a very mobile pattern, being readily able to shift its attention towards incoming sources of information.

Containing two green semi-sextiles and one blue sextile, this is a blue-green figure. Patterns with this colour combination suggest considerable awareness and imaginative qualities, but they are passive, and less likely to initiate action.

The Ear/Eye works effectively as an information gatherer. The green semi-sextiles continuously absorb facts, clues, hints, words, visual impressions and anything else of interest from the surrounding environment. These are then stored for future use in the blue sextile aspect, and can be accessed when the need arises.

The Ear/Eye is not particularly discriminating. It gathers in all manner of information which is likely to be random and unrelated. An example of this might be someone who can give the correct answer to an obscure quiz question, can tell a friend what they were wearing at a special event years after the event took place, and who can attune to the needs of others and sense in a brief instant if something is wrong.

This pattern works on its own, without any need for the individual to consciously work at developing it. Many people with the Ear/Eye in their chart find it invaluable. As always, the planets involved will indicate the way this pattern will operate. It is also worth noting that the area of the chart that this pattern spans will be the one from which the information is gathered (Chapter 8).

Dominant Learning Triangle

This triangular pattern covers a large area of the chart, enclosing the central core. Its motivation is mutable because of its triangular shaping, so the learning process it symbolises will be one of growth, change and movement.

All three aspect colours are present, giving a rounded, balanced and complete representation of the cardinal, fixed and mutable qualities associated with them.

Dominant Learning Triangle

Learning triangles are always composed of one red, one green and one blue aspect, giving them the ability to take action using the red aspect, be aware, question and grow with the green aspect, and enjoy the fruits of their labours in the blue aspect as the learning process is completed.

The Dominant Learning Triangle represents on-going learning for life. This is likely to be an important feature in the life of the person who has one of these in their chart. Lessons which dominate the person's life theme will come up time and time again, and it is through these that they will learn more about themselves, their interactions with others, and the way they can best develop and present their own skills.

The directional process of learning associated with this pattern always begins with the planet at the red/ blue corner; it then proceeds along the green aspect and finally returns to the point it started from, via the blue aspect.

Direct

If this red-green-blue sequence follows an anti-clockwise direction in the chart, the Learning Triangle is known as *direct*. This is significant! A direct Learning Triangle indicates that the lessons involved can be understood and learned in an unimpeded, straightforward way. The penny drops, things click into place and the lesson is learned and taken on board when the pattern has this direct sequence.

Direct

Retrograde

However, if the red-green-blue sequence of aspects follows a clockwise direction, this is known as *retrograde*. In real life terms, this suggests that the lesson concerned will not necessarily be learned first time around and the person may need another, or even several attempts at learning the lesson that life is throwing up for them before they fully understand. When they do, the lesson is complete.

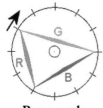

Retrograde

As with all of life's lessons, we don't just do them once and find that that's it. Life has a knack of throwing up the same lesson in different guises, and each time it does we may find ourselves once again going through the learning sequence associated with the Dominant Learning Triangle. If we do, it is likely to be at a deeper level of understanding, which will deepen and enrich our lives.

The planets pinning down the corners of this pattern will determine what kind of energies will be involved in the learning process, as will their position in the chart as a whole.

Large/Medium/Small Learning Triangles

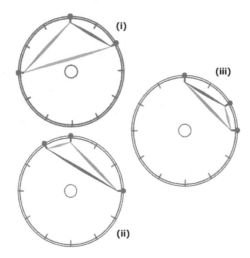

Large/ Medium/ Small Learning Triangles

These Learning Triangles work in a similar way to the Dominant Learning Triangle, but they do not enclose the central core, being found around the periphery of the chart. Large/Medium/Small Learning Triangles are concerned with learning specific skills in specific areas of life. The area that they span in the chart will be the area of life where the learning will take place and be applied (see Chapter 8).

The precise nature of the learning involved will be shown by the pinning planets. As a general guideline, the colour of the longest aspect will show which part of the learning process is the most important. A person who has a Small Learning Triangle where the red aspect is longest will actively participate in the *doing* of the learning; one who has the green aspect longest will be learning for learning's sake – it will be all-important that they actually learn something. And one who has the blue aspect as the longest one will enjoy the completion of the learning task.

As with the Dominant Learning Triangle, direct and retrograde sequence of the order of the aspect colours applies, perhaps offering insights into why some people can grasp the learning of specific skills much faster than others.

Understanding Aspect Patterns

This chapter has outlined a selection of the most commonly occurring aspect patterns. As there are over forty recognised patterns that have been researched and proven to be of practical relevance, it is often difficult to remember the detailed meaning of any particular aspect pattern. And you will, in any case, find further patterns that have not been extensively researched. It is therefore useful to have some general guidelines to help in interpreting and understanding aspect patterns. These can also be applied and used with the aspect patterns described in this chapter.

Shaping

- Is the pattern mutable (triangular) or fixed (quadrangular) or cardinal (linear)?
- What does this tell you about its motivation?

Colour

- How many colours are involved?
- What are they?
- What does the combination of colours tell you? (e.g. all red; all blue; red/ blue; red/ green; green/ blue; red/ green/ blue)
- What are the aspect colours inside the pattern? This will indicate what's going on inside, what is less visible.
- What are the aspect colours on the outside of the pattern? This will indicate what shows on the outside, is more apparent to the world, and what the person is more likely to show.

Related Planets and Houses

The planets at the corners of an aspect pattern give further information on the way in which the energies in the pattern are likely to manifest, and the related houses indicate areas of life where they are likely to manifest. See Chapter 6 and Chapter 8.

Whole Chart

Finally, return to looking at a whole chart, now with insight and understanding of the individual aspect patterns within it.

Of course, aspect patterns rarely act in isolation. In most charts they are linked to each other, by a linear aspect or by having a pinning planet in common (i.e. one that is involved in more than one aspect pattern). As we are looking at the whole chart, the whole person, we need to keep this in mind – considering how the aspect patterns might operate on their own, and in relation to linked patterns.

An Example

Consider what aspect patterns are to be found in this chart.

01.01.1965 19:50 Newcastle-under-Lyme, England

Looking carefully, identify the following figures:

An all-blue Large Talent Triangle.

An all-red Efficiency Triangle.

A red and green Irritation Triangle.

A red, blue and green Dominant Learning Triangle (direct)

Summary – Aspect Patterns

• Seven aspects are used in astrological psychology, corresponding with angular separation of multiples of 30 degrees.

• Their qualities relate to the corresponding colours:

> Orange – conjunction
>
> Green – semi-sextile, quincunx
>
> Blue – sextile, trine
>
> Red – square, opposition.

• The 30° multiple does not need to be exact; the tolerance is known as the orb.

• One-way aspects indicate a weaker, unidirectional, relationship between two planets.

• Aspect patterns relate to deep-seated motivations.

• Motivation associated with a particular aspect pattern is related to its shaping (cardinal, fixed, mutable) and to the colours of the aspects.

• Commonly occurring patterns include Efficiency Triangle and Square, Ambivalence Triangle, Talent Triangles, Kite, Irritation Triangle, Ear/Eye and Learning Triangles.

• Guidelines are given for understanding other aspect patterns based on their shaping and colour.

• Planets and houses involved give further information on how the energies in the pattern are likely to manifest.

6. The Planets and Psychological Drives

"The planets are the life organs or instruments by means of which the human being makes contact with his world. Through them he perceives and experiences the world and establishes vital and functional exchange with it."
Bruno and Louise Huber, *The Astrological Houses*

If you are new to astrology, you probably have some ideas about the planets and their position in the sky being of significance when it comes to looking at a birth chart. As a beginner, your understanding may not go much further than this; if you already know something about astrology you will almost certainly have some knowledge about the planets. In this chapter we look at the symbolic meaning of the planets in the natal chart within the context of astrological psychology.

In the Huber method, the planets symbolically represent our psychological drives. We each have a variety of drives – there is the drive to communicate, the drive to be safe and secure, the drive to be loved, the drive to assert ourselves and the drive to form relationships, to mention but a few. Each planet shown in the chart symbolises a vast range of associated qualities. In order to understand more about what a particular planet represents we can draw upon those qualities, but underlying them there is always a basic psychological drive.

There are ten 'planets' used in the natal chart, including the Sun (technically a star) and the Moon (technically the Earth's satellite). Other objects in the solar system, such as the asteroids, comets and satellites of other planets, are not considered in astrological psychology, their influence being relatively small, corresponding with their smaller size. (The Moon is similarly small, but obviously very close to Earth.)

Each planet is represented in the chart by a shorthand glyph, and is associated with one of the qualities cardinal, fixed and mutable (Chapter 4), which offers immediate clues as to how it might operate.

Another object that is not a real planet also appears in the planet area of the birth chart – the Moon's North Node (Chapter 11).

We categorise the planets into three groupings: *tool planets*, *ego planets* and *transpersonal planets*.

Tool Planets

The *tool planets* respond and act, by and large, at a subconscious level. They safeguard our warmth, food, safety and well-being. Their function is to preserve, support and fulfil the survival needs which have to be met before we can grow and develop more fully as awakened individuals. Tool planets can ultimately help us in the expression of our creativity, or if we are seeking or already following a spiritual path. But they are only able to do so when we ourselves are using them in a consciously "awake" manner. The tool planets are Mercury, Venus, Mars and Jupiter, and we will start by looking at each one in turn.

Mercury – ☿ – *Mutable*

The basic underlying psychological drive associated with Mercury is *Communication*. All forms of communication are associated with this planet, from asking questions, learning, teaching, thinking and gathering facts together in order to analyse them, to reading a newspaper, chatting with friends on the phone, writing a report, exchanging news and gossip, sending e-mails and text messages, reading avidly and public speaking.

Each of the tool planets is associated with one of the senses; for Mercury this is the sense of *hearing*. It enables us to observe, listen and mimic, and we can draw on its support, for example, to help us with correct pronunciation if we are learning a foreign language. The professional impersonator who lampoons politicians and sports or show business personalities is utilising Mercury in a very focussed manner.

As babies, we will all have used Mercury in a raw and uncontrolled way when we screamed for food when hungry, and babbled and played with sounds as we learned to speak. As we mature, our Mercury functions become more controlled, and we can direct and use them consciously rather than instinctively. When we have achieved this, Mercury can, for example, be applied to higher learning to aid us in connecting ideas together and communicating in a highly skilled way. Mercury is a mutable planet, so will be flexible and often very fast when engaged – think of Mercurial wit.

In the solar system, this is the planet closest to the Sun, completing a speedy circuit of our star in only 88 days.

Venus – ♀ – *Fixed*

The psychological drives associated with Venus are those for *Harmony and Contact*. When the energies of Venus are engaged and active, we form relationships of all kinds. There is a strong drive to relate to people and situations in our lives in a harmonious and pleasant manner; this, as a rule, generally makes life easier. But Venus can be passive, even lazy, waiting for things to happen, or even for unpleasant things to go away, as there will be a reluctance to make any waves, especially where relationships are concerned.

Being a fixed planet, the need to preserve things as they are and maintain the status quo are present in this planet's expression. Venus is associated with our physical intake and output, and maintains a balance between these two. The sense of physical *taste* is involved, with Venus driving the need to eat and drink. Whatever is physically taken in will result in a feeling of satisfaction (and possibly laziness if we are full up), but will ultimately end in the necessary balance being sought via a trip to the bathroom. But taste of all kinds is associated with Venus. We will not feel happy or comfortable with atmospheres we can cut with a knife, preferring that things don't jar and that all remains on an even keel.

When choosing colour schemes for room décor or for items of clothing that complement each other, we are using Venus. It is present in our creative urges, being strongly aligned with artistic flair and taste, and always aims, on its highest level, for beauty and perfection. In our solar system Venus is an object of shining beauty as it appears in the sky as either the morning or the evening star; it is worth reflecting on this when you next see this bright planet against the background of a twilight sky.

Venus enables us to enrich our lives with style, to develop an aesthetic appreciation for the arts, to recognise and enjoy quality in all areas of life, from fashion design to the works of great composers, and to aim for perfection. It is associated with the female libido, so forming and maintaining love relationships are all part of the drive of this tool planet.

Mars – ♂ – *Cardinal*

Mars has a drive for *Action*. It urgently needs to be doing something. This planet is far from passive; because of this it complements Venus perfectly. Whereas Venus is concerned with preserving the status quo, the female libido and forming relationships, Mars is focussed on being action-oriented, productive, initiatory and expressing the male libido. Venus might want to form a relationship; Mars is after a one-night stand!

We can be sure Mars is around if we are in a combative mood and find ourselves picking fights or arguing with those around us. Perhaps it's not entirely by chance that it is known as *the red planet*. In terms of survival or competition, Mars can be aggressive. See it at work when you are tail-gated or carved up by another driver on the road, with road rage at the worst end of the spectrum.

Yet Mars, when it is operating in a more refined way, can be assertive rather than aggressive. It can give us the courage and bravery to achieve our goals, and at its best is expressed in fine leadership qualities. Mars will help us work at things, be productive and hone the skills we already have as well as help us refine new ones. Don't expect a quiet life with Mars in action – it won't happen, as this is a cardinal planet whose drive is to do, to take action and to utilise our motor function.

Mars is associated with the sense of *smell*, a sense that we do not use nearly as much as our primitive ancestors did. Smells can signify danger – think of gas, toxic waste and, going right back to prehistoric society, the smell of large and dangerous animals nearby. Mars gives us the ability to turn and fight or take flight; our survival and safety can rest upon our choice of these two actions.

Jupiter – ♃ – *Mutable*

The drive associated with Jupiter is *Growth*, and most specifically, psychological growth. Jupiter encourages us to learn new things, and to get the *big picture* of whatever it is we are considering. It is, appropriately, the largest planet in our solar system, so with Jupiter remember to think big and slightly larger than life.

Like Mercury, Jupiter is a mutable planet and it works alongside Mercury in a complementary way. Whereas Mercury gathers information and facts in order to analyse them, Jupiter evaluates them and puts them into a wider context. When Jupiter's energy is engaged it seeks to expand into new directions and dimensions.

There is a sense of abundance and enjoyment associated with this planet, along with a liking for sensorial delights. Because of its expansive attributes, Jupiter may lean towards excess and over-indulgence. These are most likely to be experienced on a physical level with an expanding waistline as the end-product! There is a warm, open-heartedness about Jupiter, and these qualities are seen in such characteristics as benevolence, optimism, joviality and a good sense of humour. It is interesting to note that many of the ads in dating or friendship-seeking columns list Jupiterian characteristics such as *a good sense of humour* as traits people seek in a partner.

Jupiter encourages us to extend ourselves outwards, away from the more familiar safety zones and out towards new horizons where we are challenged to take risks and gain new experiences. Perception, wise judgement, a good sense of values and maintaining perspective can then be developed.

Jupiter is associated with the sense of *sight*, helping us to see real life issues with greater clarity. Then we can have a wider viewpoint, taking in much more than just the small details under our noses; we can start to develop the all-important insight, intuition and vision which will broaden our understanding and lead us towards trusting our inner wisdom.

Ego Planets

The Sun, Moon and Saturn are known as the ego or personality planets, because their qualities and the drives and energies they represent are closely allied to the physical, emotional and mental bodies of the human constitution.

It is through the ego that we identify with our sense of self. The ego planets operate at a more conscious level and we live out a large portion of our lives through them. Saturn provides structure and gives us a sense of physical self, the Moon conveys our emotional responses and gives us a sense of self through feelings, and from the Sun we connect with the will and gain self-awareness through the mind.

All three ego planets can be functioning at varying degrees of consciousness, so an important task for anyone who is committed to personal growth is to *wake them up*. Then they function with alertness and respond clearly and helpfully when we have choices and decisions to make.

Like the tool planets, each of the ego planets has either a cardinal, fixed or mutable quality, which immediately tells us something about its nature. Their glyphs are normally shown on the birth chart in red.

Sun – ☉ – *Cardinal*

The Sun is at the very centre of the solar system. Its power, energy and force are well-documented by astronomers and scientists, and we know that without it, life on earth would cease. As with the physical Sun, so it is with the Sun in the birth chart. It is the strongest creative drive we have, and is a powerhouse of personal energy for us as it represents our individuality, our personal sense of self – that sense of "I" that we have.

The psychological drive of the Sun is *will*. Using the Sun we can stand at the centre of our personality, and drawing on its abundant cardinal energy, we can direct our will to create and make things happen in the world around us. The Sun is used when we have to make decisions and choices in life, so in order to develop this planet, which gives us the sense of self we gain through the mind, we also have to understand how we can use our will.

Most people probably think straight away of *strong will* when they hear the word *will* mentioned, and can come up with plenty of examples of how the strong will might work. For example, a strong will is very useful when we have to work hard to complete a task to a deadline as it keeps us on track and stops us from deviating from our goal. But the strong will can also show up in stubborn, wilful behaviour, when we determinedly want to get our own way. If we solely use the Sun, our sense of self, our "I", in a strong-willed manner, imposing our will upon others and demanding that they do what we want rather than what they choose, we are being dogmatic and egocentric.

All the planets and the psychological drives associated with them can be raised up to higher levels of expression if we seek to apply them more consciously. The Sun at this higher level becomes an instrument of sound judgement and decision making, and we can draw not only on the strong will, but also on the skilful and good will.

The *skilful will* allows us to be more flexible in approaches to decision making. We see the whole picture of whatever it is we are aiming for, not just the next target in sight, and we are prepared to adapt and make compromises along the way. We think and act independently and with a self-confidence that inspires respect.

Good will is exactly what its name suggests. When this is engaged our Sun will shine with added radiance as we will be seen to be selfless in what we do.

Ideally, we will bring all three kinds of will into play – the strong, the skilful and the good will. The big picture we saw when the skilful will was engaged becomes even wider and more inclusive, and we lose or temporarily set aside the ego and any sense of personal self. Decisions are made clearly as we are centred and clearly focussed. What is decided upon will be for the greater good, and not just for ourselves. We become a willing agent, setting the personal "I" aside and doing what is deemed necessary. Charismatic leaders, such as Gandhi and Martin Luther King show examples of using the Sun in this way.

Moon – ☽ – *Mutable*

The psychological drive of the Moon is to express our *emotional responses*. When we are in touch with our *feelings*, we are expressing the energies of the Moon.

This is a mutable planet; its changes of mood, its adaptability and fluid responses that ebb and flow, are all part and parcel of how we express our feeling nature. With the Moon, we get a sense of ourselves through our feelings, particularly in relation to people and situations, and all too often find ourselves awash with them.

Through the Moon we express our *inner child*, and this can come out in many different guises, one of them being childishness. Perhaps we feel needy, moody, demanding, emotionally insecure, hypersensitive or over-reactive. The list could be quite long. It is likely that most readers will be able to identify with some of these behaviours – we all do it. Think of a middle-aged woman losing her temper, stamping her foot and slamming doors because she feels misunderstood, or a mature man sulking moodily and refusing to speak to his wife because her parents are visiting and he's had to miss the football match on TV.

As we develop in self-awareness, we can begin to express the emotional qualities of the Moon more consciously. Instead of being so taken up with fulfilling our own emotional needs, we can move beyond these to be sensitive and compassionate to the needs and feelings of others. Then we can respond with love, warmth and caring, and share our own feelings as well.

Our *inner child* will become more spontaneous and fun-loving. Instead of being childish and immature, we find we are free to be more immediate and child-like, appreciative of the beauty of the world around us and the new experiences it brings. Through the Moon, we express our feelings of love towards others; there is ample evidence of this in the words that have inspired love songs through the ages.

The Moon acts like a mirror, reflecting the feelings and emotions of those we make contact with, and enabling us to empathise with them. This reflection, together with the mutability of the Moon, can be seen in the waxing and waning of this planet in the night sky as it shines and glows in the reflected light of the Sun.

Saturn – ♄ – *Fixed*

The psychological drive associated with Saturn is *security*. Saturn is concerned with structure and form, always seeking to organise, preserve and maintain things within manageable limits.

In our solar system, Saturn is the furthest planet that can been seen by the naked eye. Before the outer planets were discovered, following the invention of the telescope, Saturn's position marked the outermost limit of our knowledge of the solar system, so it is not altogether surprising that astrologically it symbolises limitation, boundaries and our own security drives.

It is the planet that swings into action when we need to know just exactly where we stand – so to have social structures, guidelines and rules to abide by are all part of Saturn's realm. As an ego planet, Saturn gives the physical sense of self which we gain through the body. The structure, organisation and limitation associated with Saturn are present in the various systems in the body – the respiratory system, the circulatory system, and the digestive system, to mention just a few. The skeletal system provides a firm, solid physical structure around which the other systems are organised. As all these systems are interdependent, their clear-cut organisation is vital. The skin – our own boundary which marks our physical outermost limits – contains them all.

Saturn helps us to become responsible and reliable as individuals; if we live within the rules and guidelines of society then we reap the benefits of feeling safe and secure.

Being a fixed planet, Saturn is the perfect foil to the potential over-expansiveness of Jupiter. If not contained, the excesses of Jupiter can take us beyond the limits of acceptability. Saturn helps in curbing what might become outrageous *OTT* behaviour by giving us a sense of caution and responsibility. Taken to extremes, this sense of caution can become fear, holding us back and restricting us in everyday life, so it is important with Saturn that we get the balance right, and that we don't allow our fears to hold us back from doing what is important for us.

Because it symbolises such qualities as responsibility and caution, Saturn may not sound like much fun, and in conventional astrology it often gets a rather bad press. In astrological psychology we see Saturn in a positive light. Its value should not be underestimated as it plays an essential role in our psychological make up. Like all the planets, it can operate at different levels of consciousness, sometimes dormant and inert and responding in a habitual manner, but at its highest level Saturn will endow us with the ability to act with dignity and maturity. Then we can live with a clear conscience, accessing the deep learning of life that we have developed, and become a mentor and benefactor to those who seek our help and advice.

Transpersonal Planets

The three transpersonal planets – Uranus, Neptune and Pluto – are the outermost planets of our solar system, and are only visible with the aid of a telescope. They are known as *transpersonal* because they are beyond (*trans*) the tool and ego *personal* planets that we have already looked at. The transpersonal planets symbolise the kind of energies and qualities which we might aspire to experience and express in a less personal way in our everyday lives. This can be the sparky creativity of Uranus, the totally inclusive love of Neptune, or the transformative power of Pluto.

Most people have had a transpersonal experience at some time in their lives – such as transcendent delight in the beauty of a sunset, connecting with a sense of inner silence and peace, or finding the sudden solution to a difficult problem.

We tend to go about our daily lives largely unaware of how the energy of the transpersonal planets manifests. Most of the time we express these planets at an unconscious level, as if they are asleep, because we filter them through the personality which is the realm of the tool and ego planets. But from time to time, something of the transpersonal breaks through and we might find we become unexpectedly controversial, or indulge in power play or simply feel lost and confused.

This kind of behaviour can often be as much of a surprise to us as to those around us who experience it – however, this does not have to be so. Bruno Huber said that the transpersonal planets have to be consciously developed, otherwise they will live us, rather than us living them. And that suggests that we can harness the drives of the tool and ego planets, under the direction of the Sun, to help us work towards understanding, developing and raising up the expression of the transpersonal planets.

Like all the planets considered so far, the transpersonals can function on varying levels of consciousness – it is desirable that we become aware of how awake or asleep they are in us. They also have either a cardinal, fixed or mutable quality.

Because they move very slowly around the Sun compared with the other planets, the transpersonal planets stay in the same zodiac sign for much longer. People born in the same era, and of the same generation, will all have Uranus, Neptune and Pluto in the same zodiac signs. For example, between 1940 and 1948 Pluto was in the sign Leo, Uranus moved from Taurus into the next sign Gemini, and Neptune moved from Virgo into the next sign Libra.

We begin by looking more closely at Uranus, the first planet beyond Saturn in our solar system.

Uranus – ♅ – *Fixed*

The drive associated with Uranus is for *creative intelligence*. Uranus is a fixed planet and its energy is directed towards striving for security – yet it often goes about this by turning things upside down and causing a lot of change and disruption along the way. Not for nothing is this planet associated with revolutionary activities.

Sounds confusing? Well, one way that Uranus seeks security and ways of making things better and more perfect than they were before is by inventing and creating technically based systems which provide greater security. Our world is awash with technology which is designed to make life easier. We have washing machines so we don't need to wash by hand, electric drills and screwdrivers which speed up jobs around the home, and kitchen gadgets of all kinds which have replaced slower and more laborious methods of food preparation.

Uranus, positioned beyond Saturn in our solar system, takes things beyond the realm of known security so that new forms of security can be established. It is associated with research and problem-solving, with making discoveries and bringing about changes based on scientific research.

When the energy of Uranus filters through into the personal it can be observed in eccentric, original and individualistic behaviour. This planet is about freedom of ideas and not wanting to be pinned down. Think of the person who likes to dress creatively in odd socks and unusual clothes, or the modern art world, especially the annual controversial Turner Prize competition, which frequently causes a stir in the UK.

The shock of something innovative and different can often jolt us out of our everyday complacency and make us view life in a new light. Ideas that are innovative, creative, quirky, slightly bizarre and off-beat can be included here. The *aha!* experience of sudden insight and inner knowing that most people will have experienced is Uranus at work.

We use the researching mind to seek for deeper answers and Uranus encourages us to look beyond what is under our noses, to look further ahead and use our creative intelligence to see how the substance of life could be made more perfect than it is.

Neptune – Ψ – *Mutable*

Neptune is associated with the drive to express *transpersonal love*. Although it sounds an attractive thing to aim for, expressing transpersonal love is not easy – it demands the giving up of all personal attachments, expectations and needs for recognition or reward. Love of this nature and magnitude simply *is*. It has mystical qualities and is hard to describe, yet most people have had experiences of love of this kind.

Describing how the qualities of Neptune might be expressed and experienced on a personal level, we could relate this to feeling utterly confused and lost, unsure of where we are in life or where we're going, or falling deeply in love. Both of these experiences have a loss of clear boundaries and a sense of bewilderment in common. Neptune might also be associated with having an ideal that we uphold or strive for, or being devoted to a particular cause, or being self-sacrificing in our relationships and day-to-day interactions.

Neptune is a mutable planet, with a flexible quality that can feel like standing on shifting sands. We never know exactly where we are. Neptune, both psychologically and in our solar system, takes us way beyond the realm of security we associate with Saturn, and way beyond the mental researching, scientific bent of Uranus. We have to step out of the mind, move away from all the knowledge we have accumulated (and the security that goes with it) and be prepared to open up to all aspects of life with love.

Neptune is about identification and it allows us to connect and identify with the world around us and with all creation. Transpersonal love has no limits. It is universal love, inclusive and able to expand to encompass everything. Through Neptune we can develop spiritual identification, expressing this through altruistic acts such as quietly offering help and support where it is needed without needing recognition for what we've done.

Many people will understand this as *doing something for the greater good*. Although some might say this sounds corny, most will understand what it means because it's highly likely they have done something for the greater good themselves, drawing on the energy of Neptune, which seeks for perfect love at its highest level of manifestation.

However, every planet has its potential *dark side*. For Neptune this can lead to the individual getting lost in the mists of confusion, illusion, fanaticism and deception.

Pluto – ♇ – *Cardinal*

Pluto is the outermost planet of our solar system, at its very edge. This is the planet most distant from the Sun, yet its associated psychological drive of *transpersonal will* reflects the drive of the personal will which we associate with the Sun.

Like the Sun, Pluto is a cardinal planet and its energies are directed towards creating perfection in us as human beings. But like all the planets, Pluto operates at different levels of awareness, and on the personal level it can come out in disruptive, power-laden behaviour.

Pluto can be the masks we wear to cover up what we don't want others to see. It can make us manipulative. We may force our will on others, trying to dominate them. It heats things up, not always to our liking or the liking of those around us. Picture a volcano which quietly simmers for long periods of time, only erupting when the molten lava beneath the surface can no longer be contained. Pluto can work in this way, bringing to the surface those things we might prefer to keep hidden, yet the eruptions can bring about cleansing and transformation as we set about clearing the old, unwanted stuff that we've been hanging on to.

In the north of England, there is a term *bottoming* which is used to describe turning out and discarding the contents of dusty, neglected cupboards and drawers. Pluto symbolises the psychological growth and change which comes when we confront the murky stuff hidden in ourselves which is likewise in need of a spring clean. Using Pluto we can do our own *bottoming* as we work to bring about changes in our personal lives.

Making such changes can be a painful and often challenging process, but changes are transformative and can mark turning points in personal growth. The transpersonal will of Pluto is about finding our higher purpose in life, following a spiritual path, and giving up the need to control what goes on around us as we pursue our quest for perfection.

Once on this path, we have to surrender, give up and leave behind much of what has been part of our lives. We seek our higher purpose, and for that we have to leave aside the personal will and the ego, and trust in the power of the transpersonal will. It's a matter of *Thy will, not mine...* and although this may be one of the hardest paths we strive to follow, it is one that we will return to time after time.

Aspects to Planets

What effect do the various aspects might have on the expression of the planets they link together? The aspects each have their own related qualities; the effect is of energies of such quality *lighting up* the planet in question.

In Chapter 5 we described the aspects, their colours and the corresponding motivation associated with each of them: red aspects have a cardinal quality and are associated with taking action; blue aspects are more passive and oriented to stability, reflecting their fixed quality; and green aspects have a mutable quality with the motivation of searching, questing and learning.

Even if you are unable to remember the more specific details about what each aspect means, there is still a lot of information that can be gained about how a planet might be *lit up* and motivated by the aspects it receives, simply by considering the aspect colours.

For example, a planet that has only red aspects is going to be fizzing with energy, primed for action and ready to go at a moment's notice. Imagine a sprinter on the starting blocks, waiting for the starting pistol to fire at the start of a race. Planets with red aspects will spring into action in much the same way as the sprinter does when that pistol is fired. Their response will be immediate and fast. They are raring to go.

A different scenario comes to mind with planets with only blue aspects. Instantaneous responses are not part of their repertoire. They are far more laid back and static because they seek stability rather than action. The responses they make are more passive, ensuring security, and focussed on substance.

Planets with only green aspects will be very alert and aware, sometimes almost painfully so, as they will tap into the atmosphere of the environment around them as if they have antennae in place to help them sense what is going on. There will be an element of needing to know all the pros and cons in any situation, together with a fair amount of questioning, doubting and information-seeking.

Planets receiving aspects of more than one colour will be *lit up* in correspondingly different ways. A combination of red and blue aspects will have a stop/go effect on the planet – on the one hand, it will primed for action, and on the other, it won't be too bothered about doing anything at all. Planets with only red and blue aspects might operate like someone driving with one foot on the accelerator and the other on the brake. Such planets will have an on/off, black-and-white modus operandi with no shades of grey in between.

Planets with red and green aspects will be highly sensitised and prone to responding in a touchy, *prickly* manner. Red and green aspects make a very sensitive combination of colour; if a planet receives only these colours, their responses can be charged with nervous energy.

A combination of blue and green aspects to a planet suggests a more dreamy and imaginative response. These two colours have an escapist quality, so planets that are *lit up* with blue and green aspects will react in a measured and sensitive way – but only when they have to and when they are fired up with imaginative ideas.

When a planet receives all three colours of aspects, it has at its disposal a very rounded combination of doing, thinking and being energy which gives it access to responding promptly with awareness whilst at the same time keeping a conservative eye upon whatever situation it might be engaged in.

Unaspected Planets

Not all planets receive aspects. Sometime a planet's position in its zodiac sign is not in close enough range to be connected by aspect to the other planets in the chart. Such *unaspected planets* can indicate a part of the personality which is not well integrated.

An Unaspected Mercury

Unaspected planets appear to stand outside, and they look almost lost and forlorn when viewed against the wholeness of the chart and aspect structure. These planets are sometimes described as acting like a dog off the lead. The dog loves to run free, sniffing out the environment, picking up interesting scents and then rushing off into the distance, following them to see where they go. The owner may be calling the dog, whistling at it to come back, but the dog takes no notice because it's having such a great and stimulating time off the lead it can see no point in returning.

Unaspected planets work similarly. They act independently and often unconsciously. They are not integrated into the chart as a whole, and therefore are not a fully integrated part of the personality.

For example, someone with an unaspected Mercury might be pulled this way and that by all the interesting snippets of information milling around in their environment. They may find themselves going on a wild goose chase to discover something that has drawn their attention, quite *carried away*, not giving a thought to what it was that they were doing before. They will be eager to speak to anyone and everyone who might be able to help, drawing strongly on what the environment can offer. Sometimes they will find it difficult to stop talking, even when others tire of what they have to say, and they will ask a whole lot of questions.

Having an unaspected planet has a positive as well as a negative side. The unaspected Mercury, if conscious and well-trained (like the dog in the analogy), will return from its explorations with a wealth of enriching information. In order to perform in this way, the energies of the unaspected planet have to be consciously directed so that what is learned and discovered in the *off-lead* state can be integrated into the personality.

In the chart, the Sun acts as the director, utilising the will. When an unaspected planet is being used consciously, it can be a huge asset. There is nowhere it can't go because it has the freedom to explore and to range far and wide, and yet is able to return and feed back all that it has discovered.

Blocked-off Planets

A similar sort of problem can occur for planets that are hidden from the centre of the chart behind a number of aspect lines, particularly red ones. It can be difficult for the person to utilise, contact and become aware of the energies associated with that planet, and the field of experience of the corresponding house. This would be particularly likely if there are few weak aspects to the planet.

In the example, Venus is significantly blocked-off from the centre.

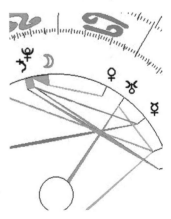

Blocked Venus

Summary – Planets and Psychological Drives

- Sun and Moon are included as planets, contrary to astronomical terminology.

- The planets symbolically represent our psychological drives.

- Each planet is associated with either cardinal, fixed or mutable qualities.

- Tool planets Mercury (communication), Venus (harmony and contact), Mars (action) and Jupiter (growth) largely act at a subconscious level.

- Ego planets Sun (will), Moon (emotional response) and Saturn (security) are closely allied with mental, emotional and physical bodies of the human constitution. The Sun represents our individuality and personal sense of self.

- Transpersonal planets Uranus (creative intelligence), Neptune (transpersonal love) and Pluto (transpersonal will) symbolise energies and qualities that are beyond the concerns of the individual ego, being spiritually concerned with the good of all.

- The energy expression of a planet is influenced by the quality of the aspects to it.

- Unaspected planets tend to act independently, and often subconsciously. To become integrated their energies need to be consciously directed.

- Energies related to blocked-off planets are difficult to harness and integrate.

7. The Signs

"The Signs of the Zodiac connect us with cosmic qualities. They are the cosmic reference system, representing the laws and order of nature, giving to the individual 'organs', the planets, a natural imprint."
Bruno and Louise Huber, *The Astrological Houses*

The signs of the zodiac are everywhere. Not only are they the mainstay of Sun Sign columnists, they are also used in advertising copy and in the naming of businesses and car models. The signs are a part of our lives, embedded in present-day culture. But their appearance in some form or another in everyday life is not new; they have been around for centuries.

The master craftsmen of the Middle Ages, stonemasons and glaziers, frequently included the symbolism of the signs of the zodiac in their work on the great Gothic cathedrals of Europe. Look up, when entering the portals of one of these richly carved buildings, and you will probably see the zodiac arching above the head of Christ, the central figure in the tympanum.

At the time the cathedrals were being built, the annual cyclic pattern of existence was centred around the tasks needed to sustain life in a largely agricultural society. Carvings of the zodiac are often interspersed with the associated agricultural labour of the month.

Leo is depicted alongside harvesting wheat, Virgo with threshing and the harvest's bounty, Libra with the grape harvest. Scorpio shows a man storing wine in casks, and Sagittarius shows hunters in the forest.

You can see many fine examples today. Chartres cathedral in France has two zodiacs carved in stone, each with associated labours of the month – on the West and North portals. Inside is an astronomical clock, complete with the signs. Nearby, the zodiac appears yet again with the labours, in one of the magnificent stained-glass windows. The Rose Window in Lausanne cathedral in Switzerland portrays all twelve signs, and the astronomical clock in Prague depicts the signs and labours with the hands of the clock showing the annual movement of Sun and Moon through the signs.

The Four Evangelists and the Four Elements

In many churches and cathedrals throughout Europe, the zodiac signs associated with the Four Evangelists – Matthew, Mark, Luke and John – are embedded into the fabric of the building. Herbert Whone writes that the particular mode of expression of each evangelist is related to the four elements through which the substantial universe manifests and, because incarnation is a fixing into physical existence, each is related to one of the four fixed signs of the zodiac. Matthew appears as Aquarius, the fixed air sign, denoting clarity and accuracy; Mark is Leo, the fixed fire sign bringing authoritative energy and power; Luke is Taurus, the fixed earth sign relating to the material plane, and John is Scorpio, fixed water, with deep visionary qualities. The Evangelists are found in windows, carvings and sometimes at the four points of the crucifix. Matthew is shown as a man or an angel, Mark as a lion, Luke as a bull and John as an eagle.

Matthew  John

Mark   Luke

The Four Evangelists
Chartres Cathedral

If the signs of the zodiac connect us with cosmic qualities, their presence in stone carving, stained glass and the fabric of churches and cathedrals was perhaps included quite deliberately by the craftsmen of the Middle Ages – and reminders of this connection abound today.

What is the astrological meaning of the signs, how do they fit in to the birth chart as a whole, and what significance might they have for us on a personal level? They depict specific qualities which have been passed down throughout the generations, and it is sometimes useful, when looking at the signs, to see them as specific *costumes* that the planets – like *actors* – wear. Some costumes will be smart and well-tailored, others flamboyant and daring, some will be heavy and weighty and others like gossamer, colouring the psychological drives represented by the planets.

Each sign costume will alter the expression, movement and demeanour of the planet wearing it.

As well as having either cardinal, fixed or mutable qualities, each sign is associated with one of the four elements of fire, earth, air and water. Fire signs are energetic and intuitive, earth signs sensuous and practical, air signs communicative and thoughtful, and water signs sensitive and emotional. We will look at each of the signs in turn, and consider how each one complements and highlights the very different qualities of its opposite number in the zodiac.

People with Sun in a particular zodiac sign will display some of the general traits associated with that sign. If there are several planets in the sign, not necessarily the Sun, then more traits and characteristics of the sign will show up. How these will be expressed depends upon which planets are involved.

The Signs and their Ruling Planets

We begin with the sign Aries, the first sign of the zodiac, and progress through the natural order ending with Pisces. The signs are always shown following an anti-clockwise direction around the chart.

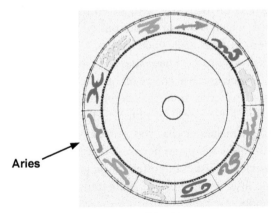

The Signs

Each sign has a corresponding *ruling planet* associated with it. There is a level of kinship between the sign and this planet, and they share many qualities and attributes.

Aries   ♈   *cardinal, fire*

Ruling planet: Mars

Aries has fiery, cardinal energy, as does its ruling planet, Mars. The sign of the Ram, Aries has the same head-down, charging-into-action qualities of a ram at full pelt. Get in its way and you will feel the full power of its butting horns! Aries gets things moving – new beginnings, new projects, new horizons to be explored, in fact anything that is new is a source of challenge and delight. Aries excels at charging in, initiating action and starting off new ventures. It has strong leadership qualities and wants to get things going itself rather than wait around for something to happen. It wants to be doing, and doing it now. Challenges are taken on gladly, and Aries can butt in with supreme self-confidence.

Because it is so focussed on what it can do, and what a good leader it is, Aries tends to be blinkered to the needs of others. This self-assertive sign can be completely taken up with itself and what it is doing, completely forgetting that other people might be involved. In relationships, Aries can tread on toes, open its mouth and put its foot in it, generally putting the noses of others out of joint. In full charging and butting mode, it will simply heave them out of the way. However, it is also capable of sweeping people off their feet with its enthusiasm and energy to get things started, which is one of the reasons why people with the Sun, or several planets, in Aries make good leaders.

The crunch may come when Aries feels it has achieved all it can in the current project, as it will charge off on a new tack because something fresh, exciting and even more challenging has come along. Because of this, Aries may leave a trail of unfinished projects in its wake – the complete room makeover that was started with such enthusiasm but now sits half-finished, the new bookcase that was going to be completed inside the week languishes forgotten in the garden shed and the report that was due in at work could be late because a new project has been embarked upon.

Aries people are self-starters, impatient to get things moving and wonderful at getting something new off the ground, but they are not always so good at seeing things through to completion. There is always an element of *me first* about Aries people; they act then move on. In spite of this, they have strong and inspiring leadership skills and are excellent motivators and initiators. Aries is very *me* oriented, and focussed on self.

Its opposite sign Libra is, in contrast, focussed on relationships with others, and on harmonising relationships.

Taurus ♉ *fixed, earth*

Ruling planet: Venus

The second zodiac sign has earthy, fixed qualities. Taurus does not like change, it seeks to preserve and maintain what is good in life – and for Taurus this is likely to literally be *the good life*. Fine wines, good food, beautiful surroundings, aesthetically pleasing things to look at, wear, listen to and appreciate are all part of the ideal world of Taurus, and this reflects the qualities of its ruling planet, Venus. In addition, Taurus likes to have enough cash to hand, together with money in the bank, to maintain a lifestyle full of such acquisitions.

Whereas Aries seeks to take action and be doing new things, Taurus is more concerned with improving and hanging on to what it has. Compared with Aries, Taurus – the Bull – is heavier, more slow-moving and steady and prefers to take its time. Taurus builds on what it has, and approaches life far more sedately. With Taurus, there is time to *stand and stare*, to appreciate and savour life and all it can offer. Having done that, Taurus may then set out to acquire some of that for itself. A browse through a glossy magazine showing off home interiors and beautiful gardens will inspire the Taurean to bring some of that luxurious beauty into their own lives. A visit – often an expensive one – to the local garden centre will provide new statuary or lush and attractive plants to enhance living space. Taurus will always want the best.

Taurus is a practical, earthy and creative sign, good at making things. Skills may range from arts and crafts, to gardening (this is a green-fingered sign, in touch with the earth and the pleasures and beauties of nature), to making and managing money very efficiently. And, naturally, hanging on to it.

Taurus is a sign renowned for its stubbornness, and here the tendency to hang on comes into its own. Whatever the issue might be, the Taurean person will stick their heels in if they think they are right, and refuse to budge – think of the Bull that refuses to move. The underlying theme of preserving and holding on tightly that goes with this fixed sign will then come into play with a vengeance, and this can prove very difficult for other people in the life of a Taurean as it tests patience to its limits. Taurus is also a very patient sign, so it's more than likely that they will be able to hold out longer than anyone else. Taurus is focussed firmly on personal possessions, reflecting the fixed earthy quality of the sign.

Gemini   ♊   *mutable, air*
Ruling planet: Mercury

This mutable air sign has an insatiable hunger for information and communication, reflecting the busy information-seeking nature of its ruling planet Mercury. It is happiest when talking, asking questions, gathering or disseminating information, using the phone, surfing the internet, learning a new foreign language, and so on.

For Gemini, variety is the spice of life, so the more new or interesting experiences and snippets of information it can get hold of, the better. This is the sign of the Twins, and as such, Gemini is most happy with (at least) two of everything, if not more. The Twins are a duo, a double act, and as two people often do when they get together, they talk. With Gemini, this duality together the mutability that underlies the sign may go something like "On the one hand, I see it this way... yet on the other hand, there might be another way of looking at it..."

Gemini is quick-witted and amusing. It's a sign that can think on its feet and simultaneously have fingers in many pies. Gemini will have a busy engagement diary with an accompanying lifestyle, and in conversation will show a rapid verbal delivery and an ability to speak on a wide variety of different subjects. This is a sign that doesn't stop still for long because it is constantly moving on to the next intensely interesting yet hugely different source of fascination. Sounds exhausting? Not to a Gemini! It is their lifeblood.

Of the new things learned and the projects undertaken, many may be scanned quickly and absorbed at a skin deep rather than at heart and soul level. This doesn't mean that Gemini is not capable of going into things in depth – it's simply a matter of the time available and the urgent need to be moving on to something new, not letting the grass grow under their feet. Gemini is frequently on the go, maybe travelling – but short haul for preference – and in advance they will have absorbed the contents of the guidebook in order to gather as much information as they can about their destination. Time will be allocated for sightseeing. Oh yes, and they will aim to take plenty of good holiday reading with them too. Most important of all, they will want to meet with as many locals as they can in their chosen destination, and of course, they will be keen to try out their newly-acquired language skills.

Cancer   ♋   *cardinal, water*

Ruling planet: Moon

Cancer is a cardinal sign, exhibiting emotional qualities associated with water, together with the cardinal capacity to get things moving. For Cancer this will almost always involve family and those closest to them. This sign feels most complete and comfortable either at home with people it loves and cares for, or being out and about in the immediate community doing something to help others. For Cancer, assuming the role of excellent housekeeper or parent, social worker or community nurse are all strong contenders; Cancer is the sign with the soft centre and the warm heart.

Cancer cares, leading with its ruling planet, the Moon. It prefers to stay connected to its roots and where it comes from. There is a strong urge to nurture and take into its own personal care anyone who might be going through a rough patch. Cancer responds emotionally, with feelings first, and will want to help out.

How this desire to help is expressed may take on a variety of forms, but it is almost 100% certain that it will involve being nourished and nurtured by the sustenance that Cancer is oh-so-capable of providing. And very often that means food! Cancer loves nothing better than to *bring on* those it is involved in helping by making sure they are well-nourished. For Cancerian you can read cook, and provider. Of course, this is a general observation about this particular sign, but it is worth checking out against real life experience.

Being a watery, emotional sign Cancer can be moody and touchy, crabby and grouchy. The sign of the Crab reflects many of the traits of its namesake in the natural world: it appears to have a hard, tough exterior, but like a real crab, it has a soft and vulnerable centre. The touchy moodiness provides protection, as Cancer defends itself against revealing too much of the soft sensitivity hidden inside.

There is no doubt that Cancer is strongly connected to the past and to its history – usually family history – and feels it important to retain a sense of being part of a long line of those who have gone before. It will hang on to the past and will be reluctant to let go (think of the crab's powerful pincers), so anything that relates to its inheritance will be guarded and protected. The old rocking chair that belonged to Great Aunt Mabel will never be parted with because it is a link with the past, and the family history.

The opposite sign of Capricorn offers complementary qualities, exhibiting the urge to move away from the family, the home and the *nest* that Cancer holds so close and dear to its heart.

Leo   ♌   *fixed, fire*

Ruling planet: Sun

The fifth zodiac sign is one of fixed and fiery qualities. Like the Sun, its ruling planet, the fire in Leo burns brightly and it does not like to be ignored. There is nothing Leo likes more than to be recognised for what it's done, for what it can do, for what it's achieved and for how well it's done it. Leo simply wants to shine and exude warmth towards all. As a fixed sign, it is happiest when others are drawn to its warmth and dazzling light. Then all it needs to do is stay put and shine. Like the lion with which it is associated, it enjoys the regal status of being like king or queen of all it surveys. Leo has a certain air of dignity; the words majestic and distinguished come to mind, together with a love of the limelight. So it is not too surprising to discover that this sign will want to be featured in as many of life's spotlights as it can.

One of the ways this can be ensured is for Leo to live dramatically – there may be a never-ending stream of exciting events which Leo finds itself involved in, and which offer endless opportunities as these are recounted, and even acted out, to others. This can be very entertaining and here Leo shines.

Then there is the way that Leo presents itself to the world in appearance and demeanour. This will never be tasteless, and it could well be eye-catching and noticeable – Leo doesn't like to be overlooked or ignored. There will be nothing flashy, but neither will there be anything modest. Leo has a knack for the flamboyant – for instance wearing a stylish fedora, classy jewels, an exotic feather boa...

With Leo, size will definitely matter. Generally speaking, the scale it aims for will be large and bold. When entertaining friends for supper Leo will go for grand and impressive. Think opulent, full-bodied and glorious, with a few tasteful trimmings thrown in and you have the general picture.

In spite of its showiness, Leo comes from the heart, exuding genuine warmth in a more open and less protected way than Cancer. Friendship is important for Leo, and once the heart is engaged, this sign will be staunchly loyal and supportive.

Virgo   ♍   *mutable, earth*

Ruling planet: Mercury

Virgo is the sign with mutable earth qualities – practical to a T, yet with a changeability that might make it feel as if it is always being pulled this way and that.

Virgo excels at pitching in, rolling up its sleeves and sorting out the kind of messy chaos which others run from in horror. It seeks perfection, and reckons that the only way this can be achieved is by doing whatever the task in hand is, itself. Alone. Unaided. Without help from others. No-one will be able to do it quite as well as Virgo, and someone somewhere along the line is bound to forget a few of the important smaller details anyway, so Virgo might just as well get on with it by themselves. Then if there are any mistakes made, they will only have themselves to blame. Ouch!

This sign can be, and often is, on call 24/7 doing something for others. It is the sign of service, of just being there when needed, perhaps even being taken for granted. The virgin, or maiden, is synonymous with this sign, often depicted holding a newly harvested ear of corn – reminiscent of Gaia and the earth, on which we depend for our existence, and which is taken for granted in our materialistic society. Virgo is capable of giving without needing to receive in turn, and can easily become blinkered and blinded to other possibilities *en route* as it wends it workaholic way towards perfection.

Virgo is its own worst enemy, and what it could take on board is that it is sometimes OK to make a mistake, or to not bother to clear things away before leaving the office, or going to bed. Dishes left soaking in the sink overnight are unlikely to bother anyone else in the household... although Virgo might find it hard to relax and drift off to sleep simply knowing they are there.

With its huge capacity for attention to detail and excellent ability to organise and retain a lot of unrelated pieces of information, emphasised by ruling planet Mercury, Virgo shines when it comes to offering these skills as a service out in the world in realistic and structured ways. Because it can retain facts, and exercises an encyclopaedic mental filing system, Virgo's ability to organise, catalogue and mentally file away comes as easily as water runs off a duck's back.

Virgo is able to teach others and lead by example in many areas of life where order needs to be created out of chaos. The practical earthy nature of Virgo means that no stone goes unturned, and the mutability of this sign means that Virgo has sufficient flexibility to allow for changes of direction.

Virgo has high standards, which might prove challenging to those in relationship with this sign. The opposite sign of Pisces offers complementary qualities which Virgo might heed and take on board to offset some of its intense *busyness*.

Opposite Signs

We have looked at the general characteristics and qualities of the first six zodiac signs, but the signs can be viewed in pairs, considering the qualities of each sign along with its opposite across the circle of the zodiac. Opposite signs can offer balancing and complementary qualities. In astrological psychology, we view the opposite signs as containing the shadow side, with a contrasting set of traits and characteristics. These can be accessed, but we usually keep them hidden away, under wraps and out of sight. Very often the sign opposite our own Sun sign is the one which we can learn most from, but it is usually the one which we dislike the most or find the most irritating and challenging.

For example, the shadow side of Aries is Libra, and vice versa. Aries is very *me* oriented. Its opposite sign Libra is, in contrast, focussed on relationships with others. Taurus has its shadow side in Scorpio, and Scorpio in Taurus, and so on through all the signs. With this in mind, we now look at the signs which are opposite those already discussed.

Libra   ♎   *cardinal, air*
Ruling planet: Venus

A cardinal air sign, Libra excels at pleasant, amiable and harmonious interaction. Soothed and softened by the influence of Venus, its ruling planet, Libra presents itself as charming and equable, like the balancing Scales which depict it symbolically. Libra provides the perfect foil to the Aries *Me me me* approach, being acutely aware of the needs of others. Whereas Aries is about *Me*, Libra is very much about *You*.

Friendships and interactions of all kinds are important for this sign, and the last thing it will want is an unpleasant atmosphere in any social interaction. Diplomacy skills are part of Libra's tool kit; it will glide smoothly into action when it sees two opposing factions locked in conflict, seeking to bring about an amicable resolution.

So well attuned is Libra to seeing both sides of a situation, the most challenging thing for it to do is make up its own mind and assert itself. Taking sides and making decisions is not easy for Libra – it doesn't want to upset anyone. So it sits – rather painfully – on the fence and dithers, being pulled this way and that. More times than not it's more important for Libra to keep the peace than to upset others. Because of this, there is a tendency to go for the *easy life*.

However, when the diplomatic skills of the Libran are finely honed, they can bring harmony and a sense of well-being to the world around them. Libra, rather like Taurus with whom it shares its ruling planet, appreciates the beautiful and aesthetically pleasing things of life. Refined taste and good quality are high on Libra's *yes list*. Wanting only the best, its cardinal qualities mean it will also be prepared to go out and get it. Libra will want a beautiful home, maybe with some fine and attractive artefacts providing a primary source of pleasure – and it will be delighted to share this with others, enjoying bringing them into the pleasant surroundings it has created and at the same time offering the opportunity to relate to others and be friendly and congenial.

As well as having beautiful surroundings, Libra will want to look good too. Expect a flair for sophisticated fashion to accompany all that smooth charm.

With natural diplomacy and polished social skills, Libra complements the *Me first* approach of Aries, yet both signs have things to learn from each other. Libra's indecisiveness could be counterbalanced by the refreshing directness of Aries, and Aries' enthusiastic charging into new ventures would benefit from some of the softly-softly, diplomatic approach of Libra. For both signs, a recognition and understanding of how the other operates would be useful as they could then both begin to integrate their shadow side and balance out any potential conflict in the area of I/You relationships.

Scorpio ♏ *fixed, water*
Ruling planet: Pluto

The eighth zodiac sign has fixed, watery qualities. The element of water is associated with Scorpio, which means there will be plenty of emotional stuff around. But with this sign we may not always see it. Feelings run deep with Scorpio; this is the sign that can both plumb the depths and soar to the heights.

There is a particular intensity to Scorpio that the other signs do not share, together with powerful feelings which can, and often do, remain hidden. Scorpio doesn't show much, it doesn't give much away, and can be inscrutable, not leaving many clues around. But be assured, there is a lot going on beneath the surface. *Still waters run deep* sums it up, and it's never quite clear what Scorpio is thinking about.

In some instances, it may be revenge. Scorpio is quite capable of holding on to a grudge, sometimes for years, before taking revenge (best eaten cold for this sign) when it is least expected... Think of the sting in the Scorpion's tail. However, this does not mean that Scorpio is an inherently unfriendly sign – it is simply the way it is.

Scorpio is a fascinating sign; it exudes an air of alluring mystery laced with undertones and promises of intensity. As well as being deep, and able to plumb the psychological depths, Scorpio has passion. This covers anything from sexual passion to being passionately interested in whatever it is currently involved in investigating. Note the use of the word *investigating*, for this is where Scorpio excels. As a sign which likes to plumb the depths, Scorpio always wants to get to the bottom of things. It seeks the Truth with a capital T. Leaving no stone unturned, it will apply forensic analysis to the subject matter in hand, immersing itself completely. This ability to penetrate, to look deeply into things and discover the truth enables Scorpio to then soar up to the heights, like an eagle, where the view can encompass ever-wider perspectives and amazing panoramas.

This sign is associated with transformation, and moving from the intimacy of deep understanding to the exhilarating peaks of knowledge is just one example of Scorpionic transformation. In line with the energy of its ruling planet, Pluto, life itself may be a series of transformative experiences for this sign, with lessons and learning arising from intense relationships and interactions with others.

The opposite sign of Taurus, more at ease with earthy material things than with the intense inner exploration, hidden depths and dizzy heights of Scorpio, can offer this sign insights. Taurus can show Scorpio how to stay more earthed and grounded; Scorpio can show Taurus how to be less caught up in the material and the need to rely on personal possessions.

Sagittarius   ⟋   *mutable, fire*

Ruling planet: Jupiter

This mutable fire sign is on a quest. Like the Arrow which is its symbol, Sagittarius wants to fly through the air in hot pursuit of its selected target. The target might be a deep knowledge and understanding of the law, or it could be exploring a variety of different philosophies, or maybe learning about comparative religions. It might easily be all three, plus a search for the meaning of life, the universe and everything. Sagittarius will question and explore, following the path of the search wherever it leads, and the more diverse the search, the better.

Like its ruling planet Jupiter, Sagittarius is not afraid of extending itself beyond known boundaries. To travel further and to widen the search for knowledge and understanding is an adventure in itself, and Sagittarius will never say *No* to adventure. For this sign, the journey and the quest is often more important than the end result, although a perceived goal is always the spur for action. Yet what Sagittarius acquires along the way in the form of wisdom often becomes more important than the goal itself.

This sign is open to new experiences because it knows it will learn from them, and there is no substitute for real life experience to gain deep learning and an enhanced perception of what truly is. As it travels, searches and quests its way through life, Sagittarius will be buoyed up by tremendous optimism; something good will always be around the corner, the cup will always be half-full rather than half-empty. Because of this sunny optimism and air of largesse, Sagittarius will attract people. They may be drawn by its expansive benevolence; like its fellow fire sign Leo, Sagittarius can be generous and gregarious.

Not being hindered by limits or boundaries can have drawbacks, though, and this sign is capable of going just that bit too far in word, deed and behaviour (perhaps especially the latter, as Sagittarius does a nice line in practical jokes). The *onward, upward and outward* approach of Sagittarius means it is always moving on – it is, after all, a mutable sign – as the search for wisdom and understanding will always be broad.

Sagittarius is concerned with the big picture, whereas its opposite sign Gemini is more interested in the small details. Sagittarius could take heed of and learn from Gemini's ability to ferret out small nuggets of information, and Gemini could learn from Sagittarius how to extract itself from being over-concerned with details in favour of seeing the whole, big picture of life written large and bold.

Capricorn   ♑   *cardinal, earth*
Ruling planet: Saturn

This sign aims to succeed. Capricorn shines when it comes to strategic long-term planning. It is in no rush to reach the pinnacles of achievement, preferring to work its way slowly but surely to the top. Like the Goat, symbolic of its sign, Capricorn will find a safe, secure and solid pathway to the top of the particular mountain it is climbing – unlike the Aries Ram, which will put its head down and charge forward, regardless of obstacles in its way. Capricorn is a cardinal earth sign, so shares the cardinal go-ahead push of Aries, but marries this with strong down-to-earth practicality making for a steady and consistent journey towards its goal rather than an all-out, now-or-never thrust.

Echoing the qualities of its ruling planet, Saturn, this is the sign of caution and restraint, yet of great reliability which takes its responsibilities and commitments seriously. This general description of Capricorn traits might not sound a whole lot of fun, and it is true to say that this can be one of the more serious, *weighty* zodiac signs. Yet Capricorn is rock solid. You can rely on this sign to fulfil its promises and pledges. It is always as good as its word.

With a reputation of being old before its time, Capricorn does tend to take life very seriously, but this is because it keenly appreciates the need for personal advancement, especially in the area of career and status, in order to ensure that both itself and its family are well-provided for. Security is all-important for this sign, and it will not rush into anything until it has checked out all the implications its actions might bring. Unlike Sagittarius, Capricorn is acutely aware of the need for boundaries and limitation in the way it operates, and is happiest when working within a clear, practical structure.

Of course, the kind of structure it likes is one that it has put in place itself, because this is the sign of the skilled administrator or of the head of a successful business which it has built up from a scratch over the years. As the sign associated with status, achievement and individuality, Capricorn will feel at home when it is in charge, or at the head of an organisation. This is the kind of success it is aiming for, and it will not mind too much how long it takes to get there, as long as it does eventually arrive.

Capricorn wants to move away from the nest that its opposite sign Cancer creates. For Capricorn, it is not enough to simply be a cog in the wheel that revolves purely around the family; it needs to get on, succeed and gain recognition. However, Cancer can offer Capricorn a reminder not to cut its ties completely, and to retain some of its links with the nest, even when it is a big shot with status and standing out in the world.

Aquarius   ♒   *fixed, air*
Ruling planet: Uranus

Think of someone you know who doesn't like to be tied down to any particular schedule, who is a bit of a law unto themselves, who has free and forward-looking ideas and opinions, who likes to have an escape route handy in real-life situations and who is perfectly comfortable with semi-detached arrangements in their personal relationships. The chances are that this person will have some planets in Aquarius. This fixed air sign will express many of these traits, and it is unlikely to care much what others think of them, either.

Independence and freedom are qualities that Aquarius values highly, and wants present in everyday life. It does not like to be pinned down, needing its own space together with plenty of time to think and generate ideas – it is, after all, an air sign. Aquarius is open to what is new, different, quirky and idiosyncratic, appreciating the more zany and off-beat side of viewing the world because that is what makes life stimulating and exciting.

However, this does not mean that Aquarius is completely flexible and open to what is new. This fixed sign may well have fixed ideas (usually its own) about how things should be done. But when it comes to the innovative approach, or to inventing and creating a new way of doing, making or seeing something which has grown tired, jaded and irrelevant, Aquarius excels. Like the *water bearer* associated with this sign, who pours out a stream of life-giving and thirst-quenching water to refresh and renew all who drink from it, Aquarius can revitalise what is old, outworn and static, and move things on to a new phase. Uranus, the ruling planet for this sign, adds inspiration to this inventiveness.

Aquarius is most at home with groups of like-minded people, so is a gregarious sign, but only on its own terms. It enjoys interacting and sharing ideas and viewpoints with people of whatever special-interest group it is involved in. As freedom, the plight of the world, gadgets and technology (to mention just a few) are strong contenders for being close to this sign's heart, then possible involvements could be membership of an environmental support group promoting intermediate technology in the Third World, or belonging to numerous internet news groups, or demonstrating about the building of a new by-pass which will spoil the surrounding countryside.

That, however, is where the relationship with others in such groups may well end. Being brought together by a common interest is one thing, but being more deeply involved on a personal level is, for this sign, quite another. This sign values its freedom and likes to hang loose. So Aquarius can gain valuable insights from its opposite sign Leo, remembering that it is fine to come from the head, sharing ideas, but that it is equally important not to neglect the heart in all relationships that are formed. Likewise, Leo can benefit from the clear and sometimes radical thinking that Aquarius offers.

Pisces   ♓   *mutable, water*
Ruling planet: Neptune

Arriving at the last zodiac sign we come full circle, back to the place where the journey began. Pisces, a mutable water sign, has sensitive compassionate qualities and, like the Fishes which are its symbol, it has a fluidity and variability which is expressed in changing moods.

Pisces is a sign in touch with feelings on a large scale; it feels not only for itself but for those of the people it encounters in the world. Feelings are easily sensed, sometimes very strongly, and Pisces will pick up if things are not quite right, or if someone is feeling sad, or happy, or disappointed, or elated – the whole range of human emotions can be read like an open book by this sign. This attribute can be of immense value but Pisces can all too easily find itself so overwhelmed by what it senses in others, that it is unsure whether these are its own feelings, or theirs. Many Piscean types describe this as *leaky margins* – a state of not knowing where they end and the other person begins. This can lead to Pisces becoming completely lost in the issues, problems, feelings and emotional heights and depths of other people, as they ebb and flow along with the mood of the moment. Ruling planet Neptune will intensify this effect, assisting Pisces as it seeks to be at one with all of humanity and the beauty of the natural world.

The compassionate sensitivity and self-sacrificing qualities of Pisces are attributes we might all take heed of in the current harsh and materialistic world we inhabit, as Pisces is more attuned to the spiritual world and can offer glimpses of this by its actions. Pisces will be happy to offer help and support if needed, and will not need thanks or recognition, being content to work quietly in the background.

This sign has easy access to ideas and inspiration that come from beyond the mundane, which it manifests in ways which bring pleasure and inspiration to many, lifting the spirits and moving perception to a higher level. Music, art, dance, theatre and film are media where Pisces shines.

With its ethereal qualities, others might find this sign vague, undecided, and vacillating. Unable to easily make a decision and awash with feelings which pull it in different directions, Pisces will find the opposite sign of Virgo offers help in the form of earthy practicality and organisational ability. On the other hand, Pisces' fluid and less structured approach to life can encourage Virgo to loosen up and take time off to reconnect with nature and a sense of inner peace.

Planet as Actor, Sign as Costume

We already introduced the idea that it can be useful, when looking at the signs, to see them as specific costumes that the planets wear, like actors. We suggested that some costumes would be smart, others heavy and some would be light and colourful. As an example, we will look briefly at how this might work by dressing a planet in two different sign costumes.

Mercury, the tool planet whose psychological drive is for communication, has a light, fast-moving and quick-witted energy. It loves to talk and gather information, and the faster it can do this, the better.

Imagine then that Mercury is placed in the sign of Capricorn, whose costume will slow down Mercury's quicksilver movements, thought processes and information-gathering capacity. Wearing a Capricorn costume of heavy, sensible tweeds, stout walking shoes and carrying a map and compass along with emergency rations of chocolate and raisins, Mercury's natural speed and nimble light-footedness will be slowed down by Capricorn's need to minimise risk and take its time to reach the appointed destination.

If Mercury was in Leo, the story would be very different. Wearing an impressively jewelled golden crown and rich crimson and purple robes, Mercury would have larger than life movements and speak with a commanding voice that would draw attention. Like a raconteur, it would love people to sit at its feet as it told stories that would be full of exaggerated details, which would be added to and embroidered upon with each new telling. In any gathering this Mercury would be satisfied with being nothing less than centre stage, only really happy when it was holding forth to an audience.

Strength in Sign

The position of a planet within its sign affects the strength of the energies it is able to express. The curve shows how this strength varies through the 30° of a sign.

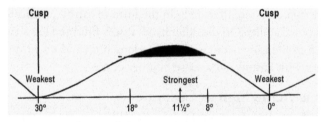

Strength by Sign Energy Curve

The weakest point in a sign is at 0°, the sign cusp. This is on the boundary with the previous sign, so a planet here has little motivation to express itself in the manner of this sign.

Working anti-clockwise through the sign from the cusp, the energy output increases until we reach the strongest point at 11½°. After that the energy decreases until we reach the next cusp at the end of the sign. Between 8° and 18° the energy is considered as strong.

This will become particularly relevant when we discuss the likely demands of the environment on particular planets, in the next chapter.

Summary – Signs

- The signs of the zodiac connect with cosmic qualities, and have been recognised for thousands of years. They are represented in buildings such as the great cathedrals.

- Each sign has one of the three qualities cardinal, fixed, and mutable, and is associated with one of the four elements fire, earth, air and water.

  Fire: Aries, Leo, Sagittarius

  Earth: Capricorn, Taurus, Virgo

  Air: Libra, Aquarius, Gemini

  Water: Cancer, Scorpio, Pisces

  Cardinal: Aries, Capricorn, Libra, Cancer

  Fixed: Leo, Taurus, Aquarius, Scorpio

  Mutable: Sagittarius, Virgo, Gemini, Pisces

- Each sign has a *ruling planet* with which it shares many qualities.

- Opposite signs offer balancing and complementary qualities.

- In considering the effect of sign on expression of planetary energies we use the analogy of the planet as actor and the sign as a costume worn by the actor.

- The position of a planet in a sign affects the strength of the energies it is able to express. Energy is weakest at the sign cusp and strongest between 8° and 18°.

8. The Houses and the Environment

"Man begins to live only when he becomes aware of his environment. That is why the house system is of such great importance to the consciously alive human being. It shows how the environment influences him and how he reacts to it."

Bruno and Louise Huber, *The Astrological Houses*

Where We come Face to Face with the World

The inner levels of the chart are all about what makes us who we are, whilst the outer level, the outside circle of the chart containing the houses, is where we encounter the world. It is here that we discover how the bundle of energy which is us, copes with the many other bundles of energy with whom we come into contact during our lifetime.

When we reach this outer region of the chart we find ourselves in the real world. All the inherited traits that helped to shape our personality are confronted by the reality of every day life. From the moment we are born into this world our planets start putting out energy. As might be expected, this may not always fit with the expectations of those who are looking after us, so we get a reaction.

For instance a baby boy with, say, a very strongly placed Mars in his chart might well be experienced by the environment as noisy, boisterous and overactive. If the mother feels unable to cope with this output of energy she will react in a way that demands that the baby boy learns to adapt to her needs. He will do this in order not to risk his security – a basic survival instinct when we are young.

So, when we consider the houses we need to be aware of this two way flow of energy – the effect that our energy has on the environment, and the effect that the energy of people with whom we interact has on us.

In simple terms we can view the houses as twelve theatrical stages, each of which symbolises a specific area of life. If we have a planet or planets on one of these stages they will be motivated to perform to the audience. The way in which they do this will depend on the strengths of that planet in terms of its position within both sign and house, as well as the aspects it receives from other planets. How successful they are in playing their part on that stage and interacting with the audience will either bring them fulfilment, or else a barrage of rotten eggs and disappointment!

Cautionary Note

It is important to be aware that the house system is critically dependent on the chart being generated from an accurate birth time as well as birth place, since the line from the ascendant (AC) to the descendant (DC) represents the actual east-west horizon at that place and point in time.

The Hemispheres

Before looking at individual houses we first look at the bigger picture – the whole circle. We can divide the circle into four halves, or hemispheres. A top and a bottom half, and a left and a right half.

Individuality – Collective

Planets situated in the upper, *daylight* half of the chart, will be consciously motivated to shine, and to achieve individuality – they want to be on top, to be successful and stand out in a crowd. However, they do need to take care that they don't get taken over by their own ego. Power can go to their head and they may use other people as stepping stones to achieve their upward climb.

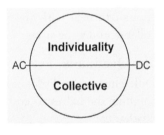

In contrast those born with most of their planets in the lower half, which we could call the *darkness*, or the unconscious half of the chart, have a different motivation – they are more inclined to live and work within the security of the collective into which they were born and brought up. They may prefer to remain attached to the traditions, learned behaviour patterns and taught beliefs of their childhood and family, as well as their cultural background.

In particular, when we find the Sun in the lower half of the chart we are more likely to meet with someone who lacks the motivation or even the courage to become the leader, to be the entrepreneur, the risk taker, and so on. Such people may develop a sense of inferiority, become jealous or even antagonistic to those they see as having real or imaginary power over them.

'I' – 'You'

Now look at the left and right halves. The left half of the chart is the 'I' side where planets are concerned with their own needs and where life is more to do with *me, me, me.* I do what I want, and without necessarily worrying about how others might feel. For some it can be an area of retreat from the hustle and bustle of the noisy world, for others perhaps a deeper journey into themselves looking for hidden meanings. However, we all 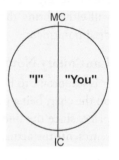 belong to the world so it is important that we find a balance between our own needs and those of other people.

The right half of the chart is the 'You' side. Planets here need to interact with other people, to be with others, to do things for others, perhaps even to live through others. But here we may also find ourselves used or manipulated by others, and we learn whether we are strong enough to deal with the world of people and work or whether we collapse under the stress.

The Quadrants

Differentiating a little more, we combine the halves to create four quadrants.

Starting anticlockwise from the AC, the first quadrant is the *Unconscious I,* the fire quadrant. Planets here are motivated towards self-preservation. This is the area of impulsive, undifferentiated, selfish behaviour directed towards self-survival.

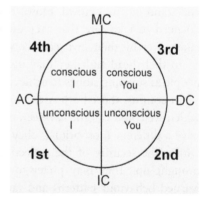

The second quadrant is the *Unconscious You.* Planets here are influenced by the people who have been part of our upbringing, whether teachers or friends, or those who would like us to be what they would prefer. We learn here how to adapt and react to the collective pressures brought upon us in childhood, and this conditioning becomes a part of the way in which we learn to deal with the world. This is the earth quadrant.

The third quadrant is the area of the *Conscious You*, or the *thinking*, air quadrant. Planets here consciously learn how to work with others in a harmonious and useful manner. We can discover how to find a useful role within society, and what we can offer to this society in public service of one kind or another. We may also choose to use our abilities in a more negative manner, and find ways to get the better of society and use it for our own interests rather than for those of others.

Finally, the fourth quadrant is the *Conscious I*, water, or the *being* quadrant. Here, planets are motivated to explore what they are capable of and what they can achieve in life, how high they can climb and still remain humble and part of humanity, or whether they achieve at the expense of others. This is the quadrant of self-discovery and this journey needs to involve not only the outer material world of success but also the inner world of our own spiritual being.

Conscious Living

It is important to bear in mind that the way in which we will respond to the energy of the planetary positions in our chart depends on how consciously we are living our life.

At the beginning of our life journey these energies operate entirely unconsciously. In varying degrees we begin to develop a conscious awareness of who we are and why we do things in the way that we do. As this happens, we are likely to develop the motivation and will to bring about changes in ourselves that direct us away from 'self' towards greater spiritual awareness, linking with humanity as a whole.

So the way in which the energies of planets in the quadrants will actually manifest in our life will depend largely on where we have got to in our own path of personal growth.

The Houses

We now divide the outer circle of the chart wheel into the twelve smaller divisions – the houses.

The houses are shown with equal size for the purposes of illustration. Their sizes actually vary in Huber-style charts. The first house is always that starting from the AC.

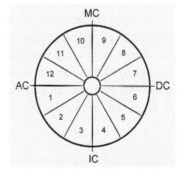

Houses in the Lower Hemisphere

In the six houses which lie below the horizon, behaviour is impulsive or instinctive and actions tend to be more linked into the collective.

First House

In one sense this house can be considered as the one in which we start our life. We arrive in this world and the only person who matters is ME. So this house relates to everything concerned with self-image. If we wear the appropriate costume, play our part right and don't upset the audience, planets in this house can help us to adapt our image to suit different circumstances and play different roles.

We can learn how to meet our own needs as well as considering the needs of others, and this will help us to develop self-confidence and a sense of self-esteem. But, of course this doesn't always happen and if we are influenced by other elements in the chart, such as being motivated more by our security needs, then we may become self-centred and selfish.

Second House

Survival and security needs have been one of the strongest motivating forces influencing humanity since its first appearance. It is here that we can experience a deep rooted psychological fear of having to do without, that can even amount to paranoia. This is primarily what the second house is all about – possessions and boundaries.

From what we possess, in whatever form, and from feeling secure in our world we can develop a sense of self-worth. Gold bars under the stairs, two cars in the drive or even a wall in our house covered in Graduate Awards, all indicate that we have acquired something and this makes us feel good – we are worth something and can go forth into the world in the belief that others will acknowledge our worth.

We need to be aware of the dangers inherent in such a powerful house. If for whatever reason we are insecure or lack self-worth, or feel that others have more than they deserve, then this house can become like a prison for us. We can find ourselves chained to the wall and unable to take a risk, or we can become greedy or miserly, full of envy and hate for those that have more than we do.

Third House

Communication in its many forms is the theme of this house. From learning to talk and write, passing our exams, to learning a foreign language. We can absorb facts and have the ability to teach these to others. This house is very much to do with academic learning and doesn't, on its own, necessarily give us the ability to develop what we have learned into something new. Here our stage is the school room, either as pupil or teacher, or perhaps having some role in our local community where we can put our communication skills to good use.

One of the problems in this house is that we may be afraid to have our own ideas. We believe that others know more than we do. We may believe everything we hear and be unable to reason out for ourselves whether it is right. We need to be wary of becoming the local gossip!

Fourth House

Imagine a forest of large, mature deciduous trees. They have their roots firmly in the ground – they know they belong there; this has been their home for maybe hundreds of years. Their roots go deep down and are now so spread out that they link with each other and this adds to their feeling of contentment. In a way this is rather like the basic meaning of the fourth house. It is to do with our own family roots into the collective. Going back through the generations we can be aware that they give us a sense of comfort and connectedness with the collective. So we are happy in a home and family environment and will invest energy into putting down our own roots and creating our own home in a way that gives us a warm sense of satisfaction.

The real drawback in this house is that, at the time we're supposed to be going out to forge our way in the world, we may be tempted to cling on in the nest where we can continue to be nurtured by *mother*.

Fifth House

The 5th house is, in a sense, a place of self-discovery. This is an area where we venture forth from the collective to explore ourselves in contact with the world and participate in the *Games People Play*. It is an extrovert place where we are likely to be full of self-belief, flamboyance and even bravado as we go out on our journey of conquest. We like to be involved with people, have a good time, and our conquests may well involve the opposite sex; these may produce the other aspect of this house – creativity, whether this be babies or works of art.

The downside in this area of life is that when our conquests don't produce the results we need to make us feel special, we feel rejected and insecure. We may attempt to possess somebody and hold him/ her as a personal prize in order to prove how good we are.

Sixth House

In this house we are confronted head on with the real, tough world in which we have to discover how we can manage to make a living. Ideas about ourselves that we may have created in growing up may no longer impress in the way they once did. We have to be more practical and down to earth, learning not only what we can do but also how to get along with others who are also competing in the world's market place. The essence of this house is *service to others*; in other words we have to become a part of the working world and be willing to take responsibility for others and work with love and humility rather than just grab what we can for ourselves.

This house also represents a challenge, because if we find we are unable to cope in a competitive world we may conjure up excuses to give us an escape route. In other words we may develop psychosomatic symptoms of illnesses that make our inabilities acceptable to us and, we hope, to others.

Houses in the Upper Hemisphere

The remaining six houses lie above the horizon. Planets in these houses tend to be more concerned with individuality and establishing our own special niche in the world.

Each house lies on an axis (e.g. 1/7, 2/8, etc.) and has a polar opposite, so there will be a conflicting pull with its opposite number below the horizon.

Seventh House

Whilst the 1st house focused on the 'I', the 7th house is concerned with the single 'You'. This is the house where we look to form a partnership with another person, whether in marriage, business or in any other area of life.

Difficulties can arise if we enter a partnership with expectations of the partner which we find they are unable or unwilling to fulfil. To avoid conflict we have to learn to balance our own needs with those of the partner; if this is not possible then a crisis will ensue.

Eighth House

Opposite the 2nd house of my possessions lies the house of your possessions – things which others possess either as individuals or as groups. Here we find the elements of society that generate wealth, as well as those who are required to protect it. It is the house of the big corporations, of the solicitors, lawyers, doctors and other professionals, as well as the arms of government, law and the armed forces, whose job it is to administer and protect the wealth of society.

This is also the house of transformation, of death and rebirth where we need to learn to let go of personal desires and be willing to commit ourselves to the benefit of society. This may also be a house of crisis, particularly if we refuse to let go of what is necessary.

Ninth House

This is the house of Jupiter where we can expand our thinking, escape from the narrow world of learning by rote and find our own truth, based upon our own experience. We can possibly enter the world of the academic and develop original concepts to benefit humanity. We can teach others and help to broaden their minds by sharing our discoveries.

But we can also become too clever with our theories, carried away by our own brilliance and find ourselves at odds with our contempories. We can shut ourselves away in an ivory tower believing that we are the only one to have the answers.

Tenth House

This is the top of the chart and planets in this house want to be on top, to rise above the collective, to succeed, to have power and to stand out in the crowd as leaders in their field. Individuality is the keynote of the tenth house. Here we need to break away from the collective and become our own person, but power can go to our head and corrupt.

The danger in this house is that we may lose contact with our roots, reject the collective and believe that we can exist in isolation. The need to retain power can lead to paranoia where there is a constant fear of somebody trying to stab us in the back and remove us from our pinnacle.

Eleventh House

In the 11th house we have a strong need to escape from the human melting pot of the 5th house. We prefer to stand aloof from the *Games People Play* and distance ourselves from the intimacy of physical pleasures. We have more of a mental approach to life and are happier to associate with those who share our own specialised interests. We like to find a career where we can invent schemes which will help to bring about the betterment of humanity. Although we don't choose to become too closely involved, we do have ideals and we do care.

The danger is that we may stand so far back that we lose all sense of whether or not our dreams relate to the real world.

Twelfth House

Whereas in the 6th house we obtained our sense of existence from our performance in the real world, here we have to look for this within ourselves. It is alright to be on our own and work behind the scenes. Here we need to learn to transcend our ego needs and give what we have to offer to others for love. We don't need to look for affirmation of who we are from what we are doing in the outside world as we have been able to develop this sense of *beingness* inside ourselves. If we see the chart as a roundabout, here in the 12th house is also an opportunity to find another direction and search for a spiritual dimension.

There is, of course, a danger that we take things too far, ultimately living in lonely isolation, losing all contact with our fellows.

Dynamic Energy Curve

We have so far given a brief outline of the way in which planets will be motivated to express themselves depending on their position within the chart circle. However, we need to appreciate that their energy will not be expressed with equal intensity regardless of where they are in the chart. In every house there will be a point where a planet will want to shout its message from the roof tops and be listened to, and another point where, however loud it shouts, nobody around will want to listen.

The figure following shows the overall energy pattern of a chart. You can see on the outer circle how the energy output rises at each house cusp, and is reduced at points in between, reaching a *low point* about two thirds of the way towards the next house.

The pattern inside the circle illustrates that the energy peaks at the cusps are greater at the angles of the chart (AC, DC, MC and IC) than they are at the other house cusps.

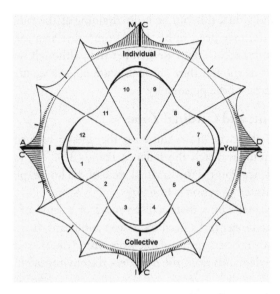

Dynamic Energy Curve

The following figure shows the corresponding energy pattern within each individual house.

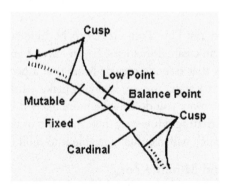

Energy Pattern within a House

Cuspal Planets

As the curve suggests, a planet situated on the cusp of a house will feel like being on top of a mountain. It wants everybody to know it's there and will be loud, dominant and possibly a nuisance – especially if there are several cuspal planets in a chart.

For the individual this can be quite draining as the energy required by the planet(s) may need to be taken from other areas of the chart – which will suffer accordingly. Remember that, although we are talking about planets as though they are inanimate objects we are, of course, referring to areas of the personality.

Balance Point and Cardinal Zone

Moving anti-clockwise from the cusp the energy intensity gradually diminishes until we reach the Balance Point (BP). The area between cusp and Balance Point is the cardinal zone of the house; planets in this area are motivated to action – to *doing*.

At the Balance Point there will be more of a sense of equilibrium because we no longer feel a need to be seen and heard. Instead there is a balance between the energy available from inside the chart and what we feel to be the demands from the outside – the environment.

Low Point and Fixed Zone

From the Balance Point the flow of energy gradually diminishes until the Low Point (LP) is reached. This is the fixed zone of the house, with motivation towards conserving, preserving and securing. BP and LP are usually shown on the chart by small dots or triangles on the outer chart circle.

A planet on the Low Point tends to be hidden from the outside world, which can create difficulties. If you have a planet on a Low Point you may think that nobody sees or hears that aspect of you, or wants what you have to offer. You are likely to make a fuss in attempting to be noticed. The more you do this the more likely it is that other people will find this irritating. However, there are ways of working with a Low Point planet which will eventually enable it to fulfil its potential.

Stress Area and Mutable Zone

Moving from the theme of one house to another is not an instant change, it happens gradually and starts at the Low Point of the preceding house. Looking again at the figure you can see that the move into the next house is rather like climbing a mountain. The closer a planet is to the approaching cusp, the steeper the climb will appear to be. If you do any hill walking, then next time you're approaching the summit, be aware of the additional energy you need to summon up in order to cover those last metres to get to the top.

The area between the Low Point of a house and the next cusp is the mutable zone. We call the last third of this area the Stress area. In its effort to reach the cusp, a planet positioned here will drain energy from other areas of the chart to which it is aspected. This will be a far more single minded process than would be experienced if the planet had actually reached the cusp. With any planet here there may be psychological implications to be dealt with.

The example shows Margaret Thatcher's Moon stressed before the MC and Saturn stressed before the AC, reflecting this lady's reputation for being extremely energetic, single-minded and controlling.

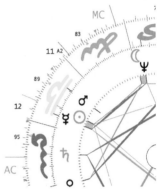

Stressed Moon and Saturn
Margaret Thatcher

The Bigger Picture

Going back to The Dynamic Energy Curve, we can see that this pattern of cardinal, fixed and mutable motivation repeats itself within each quadrant. The main angles of the chart, AC, IC, DC and MC, are the major cusps and the houses which follow each of these (1, 4, 7, 10) are cardinal houses.

This means, for instance, that a planet in the cardinal area of a cardinal house will have stronger motivation to initiate action, than a planet in the fixed area of a cardinal house. In this latter case energy will not be used to initiate anything new, but rather to use cardinal energy in a way that builds up or increases security in some form or another.

The middle houses in each quadrant lie in the contraction zones of the chart. These are fixed houses (2, 5, 8, 11); planets here, especially in the fixed area of one of these houses, will have a basic motivation related to security.

Finally the houses at the end of each quadrant (3, 6, 9, 12) will have a mutable, searching and questing motivation.

Conflicts

Almost everybody, at some time or another, experiences conflicts with other people in their everyday life. Perhaps somebody does something with which we disagree, or their ideas conflict with our own. We are aware of such conflicts because we experience the result; they probably hurt in some way. The manner in which we deal with them will depend on how aware we are of ourselves. If we react instinctively and unconsciously, as we have done all our life to date, nothing will change. The same old things will always upset us and we will continue to deal with them in the usual way.

With increasing self-awareness we give ourselves the opportunity to deal with these conflicts in a different and more productive way to achieve a different outcome.

Conflicts like these are easy to see, but what about the other kind of conflicts we experience, which seem to emerge from somewhere within ourselves? We can have the experience of one part of ourselves saying 'Yes' and another part of ourselves saying 'No'.

For instance, we are offered a new job, or the opportunity to take on more responsibility in our life. The messages coming from inside ourselves are confusing. We can experience one part of ourselves saying 'Yes, go for it, more pay, more interesting, and so on', whereas at the same time we also experience another inner message which says 'No, better not, I might fail'. And it's quite possible that the negative message will win, with the result that we lose out on a special opportunity to move forward in our life, on to new experiences.

Where do these inner messages come from? Many of our fears, such as that of taking a risk and doing something new in our life, will have their origin in childhood. All of them will be a part of our personality and we can identify these likely conflicts in the natal chart.

How? This chapter has been about the houses and the way in which they relate to areas of our life. If we find that we have planets in houses opposite to one another we're likely to find that this will be the source of an inner conflict.

Imagine that the 10th house has the Sun and maybe two other personal planets in it, suggesting a need to make a mark in the world, to be seen as an individual. There is also an opposition aspect to Saturn and Moon in the 4th house. The 4th house is concerned with family, our roots, belonging, etc. There we have a major potential conflict between the part of the personality that says 'Go for it' and the part which says 'I'm afraid to leave the nest and go out into the world'.

Which one wins? That will depend on how aware that individual is, and whether or not they can achieve a balance between the energies in the chart which are pulling in the two directions. If they don't, and they become trapped in the 4th house, the 10th house energy doesn't go away. Instead it eats away inside, and there will be frustration and possibly bouts of anger which will, of course, be taken out on other people.

We don't always find that inner conflicts are spotted quite so easily. In a way, everything in a chart has a polarity. The 1st house is opposite the 7th – the 1st house is to do with 'I' and my needs whilst the 7th house is concerned with the 'You' and other peoples needs – a potential area of conflict.

The 3rd house is concerned with collective thinking and beliefs, whereas the 9th house is to do with creative and global thinking. In one way it could be said that if we have a planet in the 3rd house but none in the 9th house there is a conflict by default between the two houses. If only one planet is involved then the conflict between those two areas of life is likely to be small. But if there is a major conjunction of planets in one house and no planet in the opposing house there is an imbalance which will certainly lead to inner conflict.

In resolving inner conflicts we have to be able to achieve a balance between the two opposing forces. Once again this comes down to self-awareness, and being able to acknowledge that we do indeed have an inner conflict, and understanding the problems that it can create in our life.

With awareness we have the ability to do something about it. Always this will involve recognising that both ends of the conflict have a right to exist in our lives.

We can't just bury one end and hope that it will go away, because it won't. So we have to stand in the middle and find ways in which, for instance, we can express that 10th house desire for individuality as well as feel safe within the environment. Maybe this could involve becoming involved with community activities and finding ways to take responsibility in a local organisation, developing our leadership in this safer environment.

Whatever strategy we develop it is essential that we allow expression of both sides of our inner conflicts.

Polar Axes

We have looked at the potential conflict inherent in some of the opposite houses. Such a tension is inherent in each of the six such axes, which are given names related to that theme. They are briefly summarised in the following, with an indication of some of the negative symptoms that may arise from the polarity.

Encounter Axis – 1/7

Egoism versus altruism. Narcissism; self effacement.

Possession Axis – 2/8

My possessions versus yours. Greed; envy.

Thought Axis – 3/9

Collective versus own thinking. Unquestioning; self opinionated.

Individuality Axis – 4/10

Collective versus individual. Conformist; rebel.

Relationship Axis – 5/11

Instinctive relationship versus ideal. Control; unreality.

Existence Axis – 6/12

Work in the world versus sense of self. Stress; self isolation.

In any situation of polar conflict a *third way* or higher perspective is necessary to resolve the conflict. What we find is that the axis at right angles to that wherein the conflict is found often contains the seeds of its resolution. For example, a problem on the 1/7 Encounter Axis, concerned with *my* needs versus those of other people, may be resolved by giving attention to the 4/10 Individuality Axis, the world of the family and of the individual making her mark in the world.

Sign versus House Conflict

There is also potential for inner conflict coming out of the two different energy curves we have described in the signs and the houses.

For example, a planet with a strong energy position by sign (page 78), but positioned on the Low Point of a house, will have plenty of energy wishing to express itself, but the outside world is simply not interested. There is the consequent danger of frustration or misplaced energies, until this energy can be appropriately channeled.

Conversely, a planet with a very weak position by sign, but strongly positioned on a house cusp, will have great demands placed upon it. It is likely that there will be insufficient energy to satisfy these demands, with a likely consequence of the suffering of the symptoms of stress.

Intercepted Signs

Another aspect of the relationship between sign and house is the relationship between their cusps – the changes of sign and of house. If we find a sign that is totally contained within a house, so that it contains no house cusps, then this is termed an intercepted sign. Any planets within that sign are termed intercepted planets. The effect is that the planet has no easy way of expressing its energies out into the world – the world will not tend to hear what it is saying. The potential for inner conflict is greater if the energy by sign of this planet is very strong.

In the example, Sun, Mercury and Mars are intercepted in the sign Scorpio in the 4th house. The subject has often found that groups ignore what he is saying, as if he were not there.

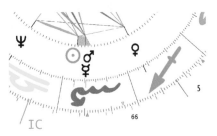

Intercepted Scorpio
With intercepted ☉, ☿, ♂

Conclusion

From this brief introduction to the way in which our inner energies interact with the world around us it can be seen how important is an in-depth understanding of hemispheres, quadrants and houses.

Many psychological problems can be traced to the conflicts which exist, not only in our face-to-face encounters with our world, but also within ourselves.

Astrological psychology can help us to understand more clearly where these inner conflicts arise, and with understanding comes the ability to do something creative about them. Increasing self-awareness can help us to change external inter-relationship situations which create problems for us in our every day lives.

Summary – Houses and Environment

- Planets in the upper hemisphere are motivated to shine; those in the lower to remain within the collective.

- Planets in the left-hand side of the chart are more concerned with *my* needs; those in the right hand side more concerned with relating to *you*.

- Combining these hemispheres gives four quadrants which correspond with the four elements fire, earth, air and water.

- The twelve houses are where we encounter the world. Each house symbolises a specific area of life. The story of houses 1-12 symbolises the lifetime journey to self realisation.

- The Dynamic Energy Curve shows energy output peaking at the angles of the chart (AC, IC, DC, MC), with lesser peaks at the other house cusps.

- Within a house, potential energy output is maximal at the cusp, in equilibrium at the Balance Point and minimal at the Low Point.

- Cuspal planets express energy strongly, perhaps too strongly.

- Low Point planets tend to be hidden from the world and oriented inwardly.

- Stress planets, in the area just before a cusp, are single minded and tend to drain energy from other areas of the personality.

- Potential inner conflict is signalled by an imbalance or polarity between opposite houses, or by an incompatibility between a planet's energy by sign and by house.

- The energies of intercepted planets are not easily seen by the world.

9. Nature versus Nurture

"They f*** you up, your mum and dad.
They may not mean to, but they do.
They fill you with the faults they had
And add some extra just for you."

Philip Larkin

What makes us what we are?

Are we really children of the universe as reflected in the planets, or are we just the product of our parents and the genes that have been passed down through the generations? Well, the answer of course is that we're a mixture of the two. The natal chart shows us a blueprint of our potential, with the house system showing past and future environmental influences. At the same time the chart demonstrates our subjective view of how we experienced the early years of our life, and therefore the influences which helped to fashion what we have become, as opposed to what we may be.

Many of us are not taught how to bring up children, so parents have a task which can be stressful with times of worry and even fear. Much as they may have loved and nurtured us, this may not always have been in our best interests. After all they were brought up by their parents, so their understanding of parenting will most likely be based on this experience. And this doesn't necessarily recognise that we are a completely unique human being and that we have our own inbuilt blueprint for the development of our personality. As vulnerable children, survival is the name of the game – so, willingly or otherwise, we are going to adapt to the pressures from those who care for us and try to become how they would prefer us to be. Many childhood tantrums are a child's unconscious attempts to inhibit this process.

So we grow into adulthood having lived through many traumatic and even abusive experiences in our childhood.

Nurturing really can have a major effect on us and the way in which we cope with life. It can affect our self-confidence, our will, our attitudes to relationships, sexuality and security. These can be beneficial or inhibiting. In order to for us to fulfil our inherent potential, we need to find a way to understand these childhood influences and decide which benefit us and which inhibit us from growing into self-realised beings.

How we go about this will depend upon the extent of the distortion of our blueprint. Many make do with what they are, and perhaps miss out on an opportunity to explore and experience a real expansion of consciousness. Those with more severe distortions may decide to enter into therapy, hopefully with the support of a therapist who works with a growth psychology. In between these extremes there will be those who are able to work it out for themselves, through their own life experience. Astrological psychology provides one possible path to help them find the way to reconnect with their true self.

This brings us back to the birth chart. We will take a brief look at the way in which we can use the chart to unravel how and where some of our childhood attitudes were formed.

When we were small we were pretty helpless and not in a position to make decisions for ourselves, let alone implement them. And we did not know how to look after ourselves and meet our physical needs. In the Western world we have been born into a patriarchal society which has been around for some 3,000 years, though it does seem as though it may now be in process of changing. And we don't arrive in this world with a clean slate, we really are attached to our ancestral roots which give us inherited expectations as to what we might find when we arrive.

For instance we are expecting that there will be a mother figure who will nurture us, and there will be a father figure who will take responsibility for the family in a more active and material way. This is not unlike the way things were in the early years of mankind when we lived in tribes. The women's responsibilities were the survival of the tribe through reproduction, nurturing the young and keeping the peace, whilst her man went out hunting and defended the tribe against aggressors.

We each have the potential for developing our own inner mother and father, but to start with we invest these roles in the two people who, in a conventional family, fulfil the task of parents. Ultimately we grow up and, hopefully, learn how to repossess these two parts of ourselves so that we can make our own decisions and take responsibility for our own physical well-being – in other words how to become responsible, autonomous human beings. However, as psychiatrist Carl Jung pointed out, when we do repossess these parts of our personality we do so with all the distortions that have been inflicted upon them in the meantime. And sometimes we may never fully repossess them.

Can we really find this process in an astrological birth chart? The answer is 'Yes', but to do so not only requires learning the theory but, more importantly, exploring the reality through looking at the charts of many, many people to build up an understanding of how this Family Model works in practice.

The Family Model

There are no hard and fast rules, but there are some gilt-edged guidelines which need to be adhered to. Let us take a look at some of them.

The Sun in the birth chart symbolises will and our mental approach to life. It includes aspects of the personality which relate to *self*, such as self-confidence, self-esteem and self-identity. The Sun can be likened to the managing director in a company – responsible for making the decisions and steering the business in the right direction to achieve success. Since we can't do these kind of things for ourselves when we're small we project our own Sun on to that person who we assume is playing this role within our family – usually Dad.

Saturn in the birth chart symbolises our physical self as well as security in all its many guises. Security is one of life's basic building blocks, without which we find it hard to unfold as human beings and make the most of our lives. Security means different things to different people – it can be money in the bank, academic qualifications, gold bars under the stairs, many friends (especially if they admire us), food in one form or another (e.g. chocolate bars), or more cars in the driveway than the neighbours have. It can also be the walls of a house which create the secure space inside, or which even hold up the roof.

Security is *form* in a multitude of ways – and we all need to feel secure. And who is usually the first person to make us feel secure when we arrive in this world? Mum! So we tend to project our own Saturn onto our mother. Although roles in society may be changing, the expectations of the new born child remain the same. Before we learn to do these things for ourselves we need nurturing at all levels of our physical being, from being fed to being taught not to do silly things that put our life in jeopardy and threaten our survival.

The Moon in the birth chart symbolises our feelings and how we experience and react to the world around us at an emotional level. It is receptive and reflective and is that spontaneous part of our personality that symbolises our own *inner child*. Have you ever noticed the way in which a baby has an instant response to every sound and movement around him as he lies in his cot? Is it possible that whereas all other parts of our personality have to grow into consciousness, the Moon is fully conscious when we are born?

It certainly appears to be that vulnerable part of ourselves that we learn to protect and which, in coping with the traumas of childhood, becomes suppressed, so that later on in life we have to rediscover it. So to complete the Family Model we can see the Moon as the child.

If we consider the positions and the relationship to one another of Sun, Saturn and Moon in the birth chart we can begin to get a picture of the child's subjective view of how things were for him or her, within the family during the first 7 or 8 years of life. It is important to remember that it is a subjective view and may not accord with the reality of the situation. After all, there can be three children in the same family and whilst the parents might appear to treat each child in the same way, each will have a different memory of how things were for them in their childhood, and this will be reflected in their individual birth charts.

It is interesting to watch family behaviour and note how a child will behave in a certain manner in order to get the reaction from the parents which accords with the position of one or more of these three planets in the child's natal chart. For instance, if a child has a square aspect, which is an aspect of conflict, between Sun and Moon it will be interesting to watch the relationship between father and child to see how this conflict becomes a part of the child's life history. In other words the child will be behaving in a way that is bringing their chart to life.

Family Model Guidelines

We now present a brief outline of guidelines for interpretation of the Family Model. These have been found, almost without exception, to be relevant – but in practice there are almost as many possibilities as there are families. For instance, just one possibility might be that there was role reversal in the family so that father looked after the children at home whilst mother was the one who went out into the world to earn a living. So, as already mentioned, understanding interpretation can really only be achieved through experiential work.

The Sun

If the child's expectations are that father is going to be the leader in the family then the place where we might expect to find the Sun is high in the chart, maybe in the 9th or 10th houses where individuality and success in the outer world are the motivation. This ideal would suggest that father will have been a good role model for the child to follow in adult life.

Sun positioned near top
14.06.1936 11:00 51°54′N 0°54′E

Positioning of the Sun anywhere above the horizon still carries the motivation of going out into the world though the goal will depend upon the nature of the house. For instance Sun in the 8th house is more likely to suggest a father who was involved in some kind of national or civic role, or maybe encouraged the child in that career direction. In the 5th house perhaps he was a very sociable individual, or perhaps he was seeking extra marital relationships.

Another planet adjacent to the Sun may add colour to the role of the father, for instance Mercury conjunct Sun may indicate a role associated with communication, perhaps a teacher.

If the Sun is below the horizon then the father will not have been a role model for achieving outward success. It is likely that he will have been more home based and perhaps with a role more associated with the local community. Experience suggests that where the Sun is below the horizon, but other planets are above the horizon, the adult will find it more difficult to realise their individuality. This will particularly apply if the Sun is low in this *unconscious* hemisphere.

In interpreting any planet, it is necessary to take account of its position within a house and the energy dynamic of the house. For instance, the Sun might be in the 10th house but on the Low Point of that house. How will that be experienced by the child? A Low Point planet cannot be seen – it is hidden from view and therefore, at least initially, ineffectual. It is not happy in such a situation and it wants to be heard so might well make a great deal of noise whilst still remaining ineffectual. In this case, father will possibly be a dominant personality without being a good role model and without earning the respect for which he is desperate. It is well to remember that the child is here seeing a projection of his own Low Point Sun which, unfortunately he will eventually have to come to terms with himself.

Saturn

A child's basic need is for survival, and he will respond to a secure home where he can feel nurtured and protected. This can provide the environment in which the child can grow up and mature into a balanced adult.

The lower hemisphere in the chart relates to the collective, and the 4th house in particular, with its connections to home and our family links with the past. Imagine a tree with its roots firmly into the ground, growing up from here. It feels secure and can stretch upwards into all areas of life with a sense of confidence. So it is with Saturn near the bottom of the chart – it gives us a feeling of rootedness and allows us to develop our life with self-assurance.

Saturn at Bottom
14.08.1925 06:19 Sidcup, England

Since security is a basic life motivation the position of Saturn in the chart will be an important pointer to how we look for our security, as well as where we might experience fears and other limitations which prevent us from fulfilling our full potential. These are likely to be linked to messages which we received from or through the mother during those early formative years.

For instance, if Saturn is high in the chart this suggests that instead of mother providing our nest at the bottom of the chart she was, for whatever reason, out in the world perhaps being the bread winner or just following her own career. The important thing from the child's point of view is that she wasn't where she was expected to be. So the child can grow up with the experience of not having roots secure in the ground. It's as though that tree is at the top of the chart with its roots dangling in space. Whilst this might generate fears and insecurity such a situation might also encourage an excessive commitment or attachment to a task in order to generate that sought after sense of security. But being driven like that may not produce a life of fun!

Through the position of Saturn in the chart we can identify messages which we received as a child, which will have their origins in the way in which we were brought up by mother. For example, the 5th house is where we find out about ourselves in relationships, often intimate, with others. With Saturn in the 5th house we may have have been warned about the dangers of intimacy and sex, such that later in life such messages can inhibit our freedom in relationships. In the 6th house we are likely to have received messages about our duties and responsibilities in life – not necessarily a bad thing.

With Saturn in the 7th house we may have grown up with a mother who wanted to protect us from mixing with 'unsuitable' children. This may have created inner barriers which later inhibited our ability to go out into the world to meet people. Paradoxically, with Saturn in this position other people we meet may see it as something solid and firm to latch on to, and we find we can attract insecure people into our life who will have a completely distorted view of who we really are.

In the 1st house the messages will have been about self-protection, such as "Don't do that dear, you might fall and hurt yourself!" So the child grows up with the fear of taking a risk, which can be a big limitation in life. And, of course in the 2nd house the messages will have a strong accent on security.

But not all messages come directly from mother. Take the story of the little 8 year old who's favourite and extremely dilapidated teddy bear was thrown away, whilst he was at school, by an exasperated mother trying to bring order to the chaos which reigned in his bedroom. Returning home the child was distraught – the mother had not realised that the child's sense of security was invested in that bear – now it was gone. The child, of course, had Saturn in the 2nd house and he grew up with the belief that nothing in his life was secure, that he couldn't trust anyone not to take something from him, and that he had to hold on to everything he possessed. The more he possessed the more secure he would be. Needless to say, very limiting!

Moon

As already mentioned, the Moon represents our *inner child* and how we experience the world through our feelings. It is reflective – corresponding with the fact that we can only see the Moon in the sky when it is lit up by the Sun – so it needs stimulation from outside to light it up. Therefore we might assume that the Moon is happiest when it is somewhere along the AC/DC encounter axis and in contact with others.

We do need to bear in mind that feelings can be sensitive and vulnerable, and experience suggests that wherever the Moon is situated in the chart it can get hurt – even in the 7th house. In fact in the 7th house we may find that other people see us as a shoulder to cry on and we may need to create safety barriers to protect us from being constantly drawn into their emotional problems.

Moon in 7th House
26.09.1944 22:55 Liverpool, England

Family Dominance

Who was the dominant person in our Family Model – father or mother, or even the child? Whichever it was probably had the greatest influence on us when we were small.

To find out, we simply see which of the three family planets is highest in the chart (with the MC as the top of the chart). What we have said so far suggests that the *ideal* would be to find the Sun highest and near the top, with Moon near the centre and Saturn at the bottom.

We have already mentioned a few of the possibilities with the positions of Sun and Saturn, but what about Moon?

Suppose Moon is highest in the chart, especially if it is near the top of the chart and therefore the dominant planet? The child may have felt that the family had great expectations of her, or that she didn't receive the emotional support that she needed from the parents and therefore had to find her own way in the world.

Moon near Top
28.10.1944, 23:45 Lincoln, England

If we find all three family planets above the horizon we may find that this was a family that did exciting or interesting things and that the child will have grown up with a good understanding of the world and how to relate to it.

And if all three planets are at the bottom of the chart then it's likely that the family centred more on the home and familiar things, rather than giving the child the opportunity to meet more challenging situations.

Family Relationship

If we're using astrology as a counselling or therapeutic tool it can be invaluable to have an insight into the family dynamic when the child was small. We've looked at the main players, but what about the way in which these related to one another?

We can explore this through the way in which the family planets are linked (or not) to each other through aspects in the chart. The ideal is to find them linked indirectly to one another. In other words, it is possible to trace a link through the aspects, but not a direct link.

For example, in this chart, Moon links to both Sun and Saturn via Mercury, Mars and Uranus. Such indirect connection indicates that the child has a feeling of support and belonging within the family, but that there is no tie to inhibit growth and eventual autonomy.

Bruno Huber
29.11.1930, 11:55 Zürich, CH

If the Moon has no link at all with Sun and Saturn, then the child may feel that he or she grew up either with no parents, or at least no sense of belonging to the family. And if just one of Sun and Saturn is not linked then the child may have grown up with the feeling that he or she had no father or mother. This may be reality through death of a parent, or perhaps one parent was away working, or separated through illness.

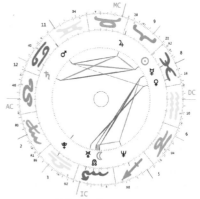

Moon Separate
19.03.1976, 14:30 Bristol, England

Direct links through aspects

Direct links betweeen Moon/Sun/Saturn through aspects are more difficult for the child to break away from without feelings such as guilt and insecurity. There are likely to be inhibitions which hold back the child from standing on its own feet and making a mark in the world.

Conjunction

A conjunction implies a strong tie. Whilst this can be positive, it usually suggests an emotional tie which is hard, if not impossible, to break without help. This doesn't mean a permanent break from the parents, it means finding a way to break the emotional attachment holding back the child from becoming an independent human being.

A Moon/Saturn conjunction implies a link between mother and child which might be harmonious and happy but might be a tempestuous relationship bordering on hate. And still hard to break from. In many such close ties between mother and child, especially with a daughter, the child will usually be on the phone to Mum at least once every week if not every day. So there is a certain two way dependency in the conjunction.

The house placement of the conjunction may indicate that mother made demands, or had expectations of the child in a particular area of life.

For instance, a conjunction of Moon/Saturn in the 8th house can indicate that the mother wants the child to fulfil 8th house ambitions which she was not able to fulfil for herself when she was young. This might have been to enter a profession such as medicine or the law. Or maybe a mother who has ambitions for the child to do well in some professional role and is supportive, even to the extent of dominating – especially if Saturn is the higher planet in

Moon conjunct Saturn
22.03.1975, 03:00 Cardiff, Wales

the conjunction. Similar situations can arise between father and child.

Sometimes a conjunction between Moon and a parent figure can mean that parent became absent and the child fulfilled the parent's role. And whilst a conjunction of Sun and Moon may indicate a close parental tie it might also mean that one parent was required to fulfil both roles.

Red Aspects

A square aspect represents Mars-like energy which needs to do something. In the Family Model this usually indicates conflict between parent and child, or even between parents. Square aspects usually indicate open hostility and as the child grows into an adult and develops a different perspective on childhood, rifts which were created in the early years can usually be healed.

Opposition aspects suggest a more hidden polarity in the relationship with opposing and conflicting needs. This sort of situation may be more difficult to resolve.

Blue Aspects

With more easy-going blue aspects the child does not feel unduly pressurised to perform and messages from the parent can be more easily accepted. However, this can enable a parent to manipulate a child more easily than if there was resistance through red aspects.

Green Aspects

Green aspects suggest an ambivalent relationship, usually with a question mark in the child's mind about what is expected of them, or what the relationship is really all about, either between the child and parent, or indeed how the child sees the relationship between the parents themselves. This effect is stronger with the quincunx, when there can be a real lack of understanding in the relationship.

Conclusion

The Family Model can be of immense value in many family situations. If you have your own children it can be very helpful in understanding how they are viewing their own childhood. This may not be how you, the parent, sees it but if you can accept and work with the child's perspective then it will help the child to progress into adulthood with less distortion than might otherwise be the case.

It is important to remember that the chart belongs to the child and that it represents a subjective view of the family situation. This may not accord with reality, although the child will do its best to manipulate the situation so that it becomes so. With this understanding it is possible to talk with the child in order to help them to develop a different perspective. Although they may not acknowledge this at the time it does usually help to achieve a less stressful move into adulthood.

In counselling or therapeutic situations an understanding of where behaviour patterns originated can be invaluable in helping a client to break free from some of those patterns which are restricting their personal growth. Working with the Family Model is not an intellectual exercise, it requires an understanding of human behaviour as well as the development of a wide experience through practical work.

Summary – Nature versus Nurture

- The Family Model enables uncovering of the adaptive, and possibly dysfunctional, responses of the child to the influence of dominant adults in the childhood environment – responses which continue to distort our behaviour well into adulthood.

- Sun, Moon and Saturn symbolise archetypal figures as perceived by the developing child:
  - Sun symbolises will and self, and usually relates to the role of father in the family.
  - Saturn symbolises physical self and security, and usually relates to the role of the mother.
  - Moon symbolises our feelings and emotional responses, and usually relates to the role of the child.

- Most comfortable positioning for Sun is near the top of the chart, for Saturn near the bottom, and for Moon near the AC/DC horizon.
  - House position of each planet can indicate the area of life that was most at issue for the child related to that figure.

- The dominant planet in the family model is the one positioned highest in the chart.

- The ideal relationship is for the planets in the family model to be indirectly connected by aspects.
  - Direct aspects between Sun, Moon and Saturn indicate possible problem areas in early family relationships, which relate to the qualities of the particular aspect.
  - No relationship indicates a weak or no relationship between the corresponding archetypal figures.

- The Family Model relates to the child's perception of relationships, and not necessarily to their reality. The child will tend to act in a way that makes the model become true.

- There are no rules, only guidelines whose interpretation depends on the actual experience of the person.

10. Life Clock

*"The Life Clock can indicate where we are in life and how we can make the
best of current influences in the light of problems past, present and future."*
Bruno and Louise Huber, *Lifeclock*

Of the techniques used in astrological
psychology, Age Progression – using the
chart as a Life Clock – is often the one
which most captures the imagination and
interest. Age Progression is the Huber
method of timing in the horoscope. In this
chapter we explore use of the chart, and the
energy dynamic within in it, as a Life Clock.
We also look at some of the developmental
phases of life in this context.

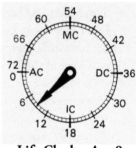

Life Clock – Age 9

This approach to timing in the horoscope differs from other more
traditional methods which consider the cyclic patterns and transits of
planets. The beauty of Age Progression is that it is a simple, clear and
straightforward technique to use, and it gives valuable results.

Although we are here looking at one specific technique, we need to
remember that astrological psychology is based upon seeing the chart –
and the individual – as a whole. The Huber chart is based upon The Five
Levels of Human Existence, starting with the circle in the centre. We
use the Koch house system because it allows for precise psychological
analysis. Bruno Huber's research with various house systems using the
technique of Age Progression found that the Koch system yielded the
most reliable results.

The concept of the Life Clock is
simple. Starting from the AC at birth,
the hand of the clock, or Age Point (AP),
moves anticlockwise through each house
in six years. Thus at age 36 AP has reached
the DC, and at age 72 it returns again to
the AC, beginning the journey round the
clock again.

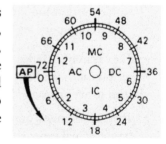

The Age Point

Life Clock and the Energy Curve

The four cardinal points – the AC, DC, IC and MC – are high energy areas both in the context of the Dynamic Energy Curve (page 88) and Age Progression. There is a huge surge of energy at each of these four points, like a thrust or push out into the environment and the outside world. This is reflected by a corresponding, but smaller, surge of energy around each house cusp. This energy peaks at the cusp, and levels out roughly one third of the way through the house when the Balance Point is reached. This is where the energy available to us from within the chart is equal to the demands that are made upon us from the outside world.

After this, the energy falls off and is at its lowest at the Low Point, approximately two-thirds of the way through the house. As discussed in Chapter 8, if a planet is placed on or near a Low Point, it may experience difficulties and challenges in being recognised out in the world. When the Age Point transits a Low Point, the individual is likely to find it hard to muster the energy and drive to participate so fully in the affairs of the house where the Low Point is. Attention and interest will be focussed inwardly and a period of introspection and inner reflection is likely to be important at this time.

Mountains and Valleys

A good analogy for the process that the energy curve takes, with its peaks and troughs, is mountain climbing. The peak of the mountain (the cusp) is a place of achievement, high energy output and high profile recognition; the valley you stand in (the Low Point) looking up towards the peak of the mountain you are going to climb, is a place of gathering your resources, planning your strategy and route, biding your time and connecting with your innermost aspirations.

In astrological psychology, the *psychological houses* span the distance from one Low Point to the next. For example when we are at the Low Point of the 5th house, we are already looking ahead and getting more interested and involved in the matters of the 6th house.

As the mountain climbing analogy is a useful one to describe the journey of the Age Point through the houses, perhaps you could now imagine that you are in a valley and that you can see a mountain ahead of you. Your thoughts are focussed on getting to the top of the mountain because you know there will be a wonderful view when you get there, and that is the place you want to be. Then you start to look around you at the valley and realise how far off the distant mountain top is.

You know it's going to be very hard work to reach the peak but you also know that if you stay in the valley, no-one will take any notice of you, or recognise you, or hear you. So off you set. You notice how steep the climb to the top is likely to be, but you are determined to get there anyway.

Cast your mind back to any hills or peaks that you might have climbed, and you will get a sense of the psychological movement of the Age Point when it is moving from Low Point to cusp in your own chart and life journey. It can feel like hard work. The toughest and most difficult part of the climb is usually just before you reach the top. The mountain peak is in sight, but as you are still not quite there, a supreme last burst of effort and energy is required in the final stage of the ascent.

When you reach the top there is a great feeling of elation and achievement. You can see for miles, there's a wonderful view, and you might even want to put a stake in the ground with a sign on it saying "I did it!" There is a feeling of power, pride and achievement; this corresponds to the feelings we can have when our Age Point is on the cusp of a house. There is a sense of being able to connect strongly and powerfully with the world as our energy output is high, and we are ready and willing to participate in worldly affairs.

Staying with this analogy, consider what happens when you've had a breather, have drunk in the view, eaten your sandwiches and had a cup of tea from your flask on the top of this mountain. You decide that it's time to start back down the other side, and this time it's easy because you can move much faster going down hill. The energy flows swiftly and easily once you are over the peak. In the chart it is similar once we get over the cusp and enter the cardinal zone of the next house. Then you reach a plateau, there is less need to move so fast as the terrain levels out and you can walk in a more measured way. In the chart this corresponds to the Balance Point and the fixed zone of the house.

On your journey down the mountainside, you eventually reach the next valley, and likewise in the chart, you will arrive at the next Low Point where you will pause and stay for a while before moving out again into the mutable zone which will take you up towards the next cusp.

This pattern of dynamic energy is at work as our age progresses around the chart and it corresponds to the way the hand of Life Clock ticks around the chart. Using Age Progression you can be aware that at some phases in life you will be climbing up what feels like a mountain, and this can be really hard work.

At other times, life will be exhilarating, corresponding to when you've reached the mountain top. Then you will coast for a while, and eventually reach the Balance Point.

At this place you will not need to put out excessive amounts of energy as everything is smoother and easier; you might feel as if you've really got it all together in an efficient way. This point of the dynamic curve could be likened to juggling whilst standing on one leg twirling a hoop around your ankle at same time. Everything is streamlined.

After a while, you find that you start to drop a few of the juggling balls, and maybe you trip yourself up with a hoop; this usually signifies that you have hit the Low Point.

Age Point at the Low Point

Reaching the Low Point is an important and significant psychological stage. When we reach the Low Point in a house, it can be a time of inner reflection, of taking stock of all the life experiences that have gone before, of reconnecting with the circle in the centre of the chart, the meeting place of our personal and transpersonal self. Many people find that the Low Point experience offers opportunities for getting in touch with the soul's purpose.

Counsellors working with astrological psychology often find that clients will seek help and clarification of their life journey when they reach a Low Point. When the hand of the Life Clock moves over a Low Point, things in the outside world might feel like hard work. The experience can be tough and might include, for example, losing your job, getting depressed, or finding a relationship is splitting up. We might start to question what we are here for, and ask "What is the purpose of my life?" That question often accompanies the Low Point experience, because Low Points are like crossroads where people stop and ponder on the question "Where do I go from here?" They are, in effect, opportunities to reassess what life is about.

The time the Age Point takes to travel from the cusp to the Balance Point is 2 years and 3 months, and that from the cusp to the Low Point is 3 years and 8 months.

Movement of the Age Point

The hand of the Life Clock starts moving when we are born, beginning at the ascendant, which marks the starting point of the whole chart. Travelling in an anti-clockwise direction around the chart, the hand of the Life Clock takes 6 years to move through each of the twelve houses of the chart, taking 72 years to complete one full circuit. So at 6 years of age, the hand of the Life Clock is at the 2nd house cusp, at 12 years it is at the 3rd house cusp and so on, all the way around the chart.

As it moves around the chart, the hand of the Life Clock will point to the planets, making aspects to them for the entire span of the 72 years, offering different experiences and opportunities for deeper understanding and personal growth as it does so. When it returns to the ascendant, it continues on round the chart again, presenting the same opportunities, but with the added weight of much understanding and experience behind them.

Some Significant Ages

The ages that correspond with the four cardinal points are of particular significance. The moment of birth coincides with the AC, the starting point of the chart where the zodiac and the eastern horizon meet. Birth is a critical time for us all. We are pushed out into the world and we have to survive. Our entry into life corresponds with the surge of energy coming from the centre of the chart, shown graphically in the diagram.

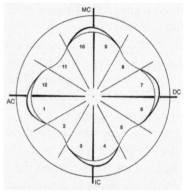

Energy Surge at Cardinal Points

Continuing in an anti-clockwise direction, we come to age 18 and the IC, where there is another surge of energy. This is the age when many young people feel the need to push out into the world and go their own way. They leave school or home and begin to establish a more independent existence for themselves.

At age 36, when the hand of the Life Clock reaches the DC, a long period of self-development, beginning with the birth of the individual, is complete. Here the person confronts the world around them and compares him or herself against what they see there. At this age there is often an awakening, of coming into a new kind of conscious awareness and an excitement that life holds more in store than might have been thought possible.

At age 54 the MC is reached. This marks the culmination point of the chart. It is the highest point, where maturity, status, standing and recognition of self are likely to be the uppermost issues. The person is able to stand alone as an individual in their own right, and acknowledge, with a sense of achievement and satisfaction, the fact that they have made the journey to this point in life.

House Size Matters

The speed of the Age Point is constant; 6 years per house. But the size of the house needs to be considered. Travelling through a small house, the Age Point moves slowly. The experience in our own life journey of moving through a small house can be quite intense. Events will make a deeper and longer-lasting impression via the planets that the Age Point passes, or the aspects that it makes to other planets.

Travelling through a large house, the Age Point seems to move faster and it may feel like a lot is going on. Life will be busy, even hectic. But although the individual may experience more things happening, these events will be touched on in less depth and intensity as there is less time for them to make a deep impression. In a large house, the Age Point seems to get its skates on and it moves fast.

Psychological Life Phases

Each house has an overall psychological theme. There are thus twelve such themes, related to different phases of life, as shown in the following.

1st house, age 0-6: Formation of the "I"

2nd house, age 6-12: Creation of life and awareness of possessions

3rd house, age 12-18: Learning and education

4th house, age 18-24: Detaching from parental home

5th house, age 24-30: Testing out life experiences

6th house, age 30-36: Coping with and establishing existence

7th house, age 36-42: Intense outward focus, relationships, partners

8th house, age 42-48: Transformation and rebirth; mid-life crisis

9th house, age 48-54: Formation of individual life philosophy

10th house, age 54-60: Authority, individuation, self-realisation

11th house, age 60-66: Freely chosen friends and relationships

12th house, age 66-72: Introversion, solitude

Within each house can also be identified three distinct sub-phases, corresponding with the cardinal, fixed and mutable zones of the house, giving 36 distinct psychological life phases in total.

The theme of 1st house, for example, is about the formation of the sense of "I" and of the young child establishing a separate identity from it's mother. A young baby's development covers a considerable distance from birth to 6 years of age. The first 6 years of life is about finding their own feet, both literally and psychologically, and mastering their environment sufficiently to allow them to live independently.

The 1st house is the natural house of the sign of Aries, so there is a lot of *Me, me* around, accompanied by expressions of independence in the form of temper tantrums whilst the process of awakening and stabilising the sense of a personal "I" takes place. How the child goes about this will be coloured and influenced by any planets in the 1st house. If Mars is there, expect ructions when the Age Point is conjunct this planet; if Venus or the Moon is there, things might be somewhat gentler.

Another example is the movement of the Age Point through the 6th house which covers ages 30 to 36. This particular life phase is about coping with and establishing our existence. It is often the time when someone is setting themselves up in the realm of work, trying to establish themselves in their job. A career path is being laid down. The 6th house is associated with work and being of service, so when the Age Point enters it, issues relevant to this specific psychological life phase and the activities that go with it will be uppermost. Within this phase, there will be stages where the individual will want to assert themselves in order to justify their existence.

It might be a time of changing jobs, or of moving from one profession to another, and it may be that this change has to be made right now as the individual will not know when they will be able to do it in the future. The mid-thirties are approaching, and perhaps there are already family and mortgage commitments, so this period of life is the optimum time to sort out any professional issues. At age 34, the Low Point of the 6th house is reached, a time when people often make life-changing decisions. This is in preparation for meeting one of the cardinal points in the chart, at age 36. And this can be a major event when we realise that there is much more to life than we had ever previously imagined.

Arriving here at the DC, we see ourselves through the eyes of other people. We move into the 7th house and enter the psychological life phase which is concerned with one-to-one relationships and encounters.

We gain a far stronger sense of ourselves through our interactions with others, and we learn about ourselves from what they mirror back to us. This is an important turning point. As the Age Point travels through the 7th house, if there are any problems with partnerships or relationships, this period of life is the optimum time to deal with them. The Low Point at around age 40 brings the potential for partnership crisis and a revision of lifestyle, so it could be a time of make or break – whatever the issues are, they will either get resolved because we stick with it and work it through, or the partnership may end.

Mid-Life Crisis

The 8th house is very significant. The 8th house Low Point is also the psychological Low Point of the whole chart. This occurs between the ages of 45 and 46; the mid-forties coinciding with the classic age of the mid-life crisis. Very often people face all manner of challenges and have life changing experiences at this Low Point. The psychological life phase is one of transformation and rebirth.

From around age 42 onwards, there is a new orientation in marriage or partnerships, in family commitments and in professional life. By this age most women will have had their children and are starting to think about either returning to work or doing something new or different which will incorporate their own needs and interests as well as those of their family. There may also be a period of utter boredom and teeth-gnashing frustration, for women and men alike, when they ask themselves "What am I doing with my life? I'm doing the same thing day in, day out. What is the point of it all?"

Big changes can be made at this stage. Many people at this Low Point change their job; some leave the relationship they're in. They may feel that their environment challenges them to consider what they are doing with their lives, and this forces them to assess how satisfying things are for them in reality. At every Low Point we are closer to the soul's purpose, but even more so during the intense Low Point experience in the 8th house. We are more keenly attuned to take heed of our inner voice, and to act upon the guidance which comes from within. We connect with what is coming from the circle in the centre of the chart, and we begin to question what we are doing, why we are doing it. We know that changes need to be made.

When we understand the psychological life phases, it's easier to manage the bad or difficult patch we happen to be going through. We can see that it's just that – a phase – and that it is not going to go on indefinitely. Issues that are intense and uppermost at the time do pass. Time moves on; hopefully we, engaging our will, can also move on. But the chances are that if we don't grasp the nettle, meet the challenges that arise at this point in time and deal with them, they will come back again at a later date and demand our attention.

Duration of the Low Point experience

The experiences and the period of introspection at a Low Point may last for anything up to a year, possibly starting up to eight months beforehand. It's possible that we could feel intermittently edgy, disorientated, restless, uncertain and uncomfortable during this time.

Change of Sign

The sign the Age Point is moving through is also important. The sign offers a backdrop and flavours the setting of the main life experiences at this time. This quality will influence experience of the planets which are aspected and the area of the Dynamic Energy Curve that the Age Point is moving through.

A change of sign can be significant. Moving from a fire to an earth sign will indicate a subtle shift away from the enthusiastic initiation of new projects, to a greater emphasis on the consolidation and completion of things which have been started. The move from an earth to an air sign will signify a lightening up, with perhaps less emphasis on practical matters and more on communication and learning. The change from an air to a water sign is likely to herald the start of a more sensitive, feeling and emotional phase. And the change from a water to a fire sign is likely to signal a return to a more initiatory pattern.

Age Point in Aspect to Planets

Aspects from Age Point to the planets are of great importance, particularly the conjunction and the opposition.

Conjunctions give immediate, direct and total experience of the planet involved. At this time the drives associated with the planet are likely to figure strongly in the person's life, and come into sharp focus. Such events in the first eighteen years of life are likely to relate to significant formative experiences.

Oppositions similarly connect with the energies of the planet, but at a distance, bringing the feeling of events happening to us which are slightly out of our control. There is no way you can wriggle out from an opposition from a planet. If you do, the theme that the planet represents will simply come back again in a different way when the Age Point makes another aspect to it. The square and the quincunx can be particularly powerful in this respect. Generally the other aspects tend to be of less significance than the conjunction and opposition.

If the Age Point is making an aspect to a planet in one of the aspect patterns, this is likely to trigger the entire pattern and bring its associated behaviour to the fore in the person's life.

Those familiar with astrology may wonder how Age Progression relates to astrological transits and progressions. The Hubers' researches suggest that Age Progression is the most significant effect, the others being of secondary importance.

Example – A Real Life Experience of Age Progression

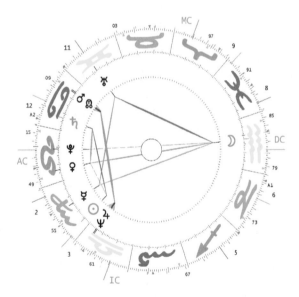

19.09.1945, 02:30 Tadcaster, England

In this chart, the conjunction of the Age Point with Venus in the 1st house, in Leo, coincided with this woman's first experiences of going to stage dancing classes, and appearing in various productions, complete with pretty sparkly costumes to wear, which at the age of 4, she – with Venus in Leo – loved to dress up in. Her mother had taken her to these classes to help improve her confidence (she was described as shy). This was a potentially helpful thing to have experienced during the 1st house/ formation of the "I" phase of life.

Oppositions of the Age Point to planets are powerful, and can be experienced as more like something happening to you, as if coming from afar, and which is slightly out of your control. Her Age Point in the 8th house opposite Mercury was a time when this woman was overwhelmed with paperwork, form-filling, phone calls, communication of all kinds and frequent travelling. Her father was taken ill and had to live in a nursing home. She had to make arrangements with Social Services and the nursing home, covering all aspects of his care and how this was to be funded, in addition to travelling some 400 miles each week to visit him.

This opposition triggered the Large Learning Triangle which dominates the chart, bringing new learning and experiences into her life – she'd never had to deal with a situation like this before. Her Moon, part of this aspect pattern, was fully engaged as well; it was a time of reconnecting with childhood memories, and from an adult perspective, she once again experienced the father/daughter relationship. Her father worsened and died a few months later, whilst her Age Point was on the Low Point of the 8th house. She had to learn to let go, move on and transform her life, bringing something new into it.

Five months later she took on, and successfully ran her own business, something she had never done before. It is interesting to note that her Age Point was moving through Pisces, encouraging emotional issues to come to the surface, and also to see that the 8th house is small, so the experiences she had during this period of time were intense.

Open Spaces

Open spaces in the chart's aspect structure can be deceptive. The above chart shows apparently nothing going on between the Age Point conjunction with Jupiter/Neptune that would have taken place at age 14, and the conjunction with the Moon at age 37. Yet when the psychological life phases, the size of houses, the sign changes, the movement of the Age Point across several Low Points and several cusps, plus the many aspects the Age Point made to other planets in the chart are considered (amongst them several oppositions), it can be appreciated that with Age Progression, something is always happening.

Summary – Life Clock

- Age Progression is the Huber method of timing in the horoscope.

- Age Point moves anticlockwise from AC at birth, taking 6 years to move through each house.

- There is a surge of outward energy at the cardinal points AC, DC, MC, IC , and to a lesser degree at other house cusps.

- At the Low Points energy and attention are more directed inward – periods of reflection and taking stock.

   The 8th house Low Point is of particular significance, corresponding with the Low Point of the whole chart and the traditional 'mid-life crisis'.

- Each house is associated with a corresponding psychological life phase.

- Life experience through small houses can be intense; large houses can be eventful and hectic but with shallower experiences.

- Age Point passing through a change of sign can signal a corresponding change in the quality of psychological life experience.

- Conjunction or opposition of Age Point with a planet emphasises experience of those planetary energies, and of related aspect patterns. Other aspects can also be significant, to a lesser degree.

11. Psychological and Spiritual Growth

"A human being must be born twice. Once from his mother, and again from his own body and his own existence. The body is like an egg, and the essence of man must become a bird in that egg through the warmth of love, and then he can escape from his body and fly in the eternal world of the soul beyond time and space."

Sultan Walad, son of Rumi

The whole of this book is about using astrology to facilitate the psychological and spiritual growth of the human being, within the context of the spiritual evolution of humanity (Chapter 2). Now we recap on the astrological features covered so far, in the context of this growth process, and introduce some further considerations.

Reincarnation and Karma

In their book *Transformation: Astrology as a Spiritual Path*, Bruno and Louise Huber suggest that the theories of reincarnation and karma that came from eastern philosophies provide a model that is consistent with their astrological insights. In its journey through many lifetimes the soul seeks to perfect itself and achieve reunion with the source from whence it came. Karma is accumulated as acts are done through ignorance and injustice, until through increasing awareness and raising consciousness it is slowly dissipated again, removing the barrier to reunion.

The signs of the zodiac symbolise this journey of the soul over many lifetimes. We describe this here only in its barest essence.

In Aries the idea of the individual is formed; in Taurus the desire nature develops; in Gemini comes the first sense of duality; and in Cancer the individual person is created as part of the collective.

In Leo the person blossoms as a self willed individual; in Virgo there is service to others; and in Libra a balance is achieved between them.

In Scorpio comes the crisis of death of old patterns and rebirth with the new, leading to the emergence of the self-driven spiritual orientation of Sagittarius.

In Capricorn comes initiation into full spiritual power and authority; in Aquarius the material and spiritual are held in harmonious balance; and in Pisces is the return to the Father's home – the ultimate enlightenment.

Louise Huber's book *Reflections and Meditations on the Signs of the Zodiac* gives deep insight into the signs, to the crises that those born under specific signs are likely to experience, and to the connection through meditation with the energies of particular signs as the Sun follows its annual path through the zodiac.

Stages of Development

When we come to consider the soul's incarnation in a particular lifetime, Andrew Harvey gives us a simple model of the four stages through which the human being grows (in his book *The Way of Passion* on the Sufi mystic Jalal-ud-Din Rumi.)

The first stage is in early childhood, when in varying degrees we still retain an innocence and sense of connection with our divine origin. But soon the child is assailed by wounds, terrors, conventions of society and expectations of family members, and probably also by the subconscious karma from previous lifetimes.

A *false self* is created for stage 2 – an ego that adapts to handle those wounds and terrors and live up to the expectations of family and society. Much of this structure of sub-personalities is built to cope with or repress the fears invoked by those childhood experiences. Many people live the whole of their lives at this stage, developing and thickening this ego structure along the way.

Modern western culture as portrayed in the mass media is a *stage 2 culture* – trapped in an endless round of posturing egos, pleasure seeking, quiet desperation, and gradual deterioration of the material environment that is its focus.

Often, the move beyond stage 2 is precipitated by a breakdown, a *spiritual experience*, special dreams or an increasing feeling of dissatisfaction and inauthenticity. In stage 3 the *false self* is slowly uncovered, and we can begin to strip away the unnecessary constructions of the ego that were established in ignorance, simply to enable us to cope. This is a long drawn out process, and few reach the end of this stage during their lives, but many make good progress along the way.

Astrological psychology can help us to move beyond stage 2 and make progress through this long third stage.

At stage 4 Harvey indicates that "the direct vision of the divine nature of Reality" is achieved, and the false self has been largely transcended. This stage has its own "subtle agonies" and leads eventually to enlightenment, such as that of the Buddha or Rumi.

Psychological and Spiritual

On page 4 we introduced Assagioli's Egg Model of the individual psyche, showing the conscious personal self at the centre, surrounded by its field of conscious awareness and various levels of the unconscious. This view of the spiritual nature of man pervades the Huber approach to astrological psychology. This model itself is said to be based on the Qabalistic *tree of life*, the model of the spiritual reality of the human being that comes to us from ancient times.

At the top of the Egg is the *Higher Self*, the link with the divine/ spiritual nature. At Harvey's stage 4 this link has been established. On page 12 we saw that the central core of the chart symbolises this inner spiritual essence.

Our task at stage 3 is in essence two-fold, potentially proceeding in parallel. The first task is essentially psychological, within the Egg. All those unconscious patterns and unhealthy adaptations/ sub-personalities that vie to take control of the ego need to be uncovered and resolved, so that an autonomous coherent integrated personality can be developed.

The second task is essentially spiritual, transcending the confines of the Egg. The autonomous personality is purified and begins to live according to spiritual values, developing a relationship with the Higher Self/ spiritual/ divine. The ego begins to cede control to the soul.

The birth chart can give insight into both of these tasks of the individual's growth process, and the blockages to progress. We can now profitably revisit many of the features covered in earlier chapters, highlighting their relevance, and presenting some new material to enhance our understanding.

Unconscious Motivations

In Chapter 4 and Chapter 5 we saw how the aspect structure and patterns surrounding the central core can give strong clues to our unconscious motivations. These clues can help highlight the ingrained patterns that may be holding us back from growth, and they can also identify the potentials that we have so far excluded from our current field of experience.

Psychological Drives

In Chapter 6 we saw how the planets represent our basic psychological drives, in the three categories of tool planets, ego planets and transpersonal planets. Potential problems have been identified for the expression of planetary energies, notably: Low Point, Blocked, Stressed and Intercepted planets. Such planets are likely to highlight particular problems and patterns of the personality, often associated with unconscious debilitating fears.

When Age Point comes into aspect with such planets this can often highlight these problems/ fears, at the same time giving the opportunity for their resolution.

Levels of Consciousness

In terms of the personal growth process it is immediately apparent that the ego planets will play an important role in the process of integrating the individual psyche, and the transpersonal planets may reflect some sense of the goal and final achievement of the ultimate spiritual alignment.

However, it is not quite as simple as this. The functions represented by all the planets are still present in the spiritually advanced individual, but they are operating at a higher level. The functions represented by the transpersonal planets are present in even the most criminally-minded individual, but operating at a lower level.

The descriptions in Chapter 6 give some indications of the planets operating at different levels, depending on our degree of self awareness and spiritual development.

For simplicity, we can categorise these levels as *asleep, waking,* and *awake,* roughly corresponding with Harvey's stages 2, 3 and 4 respectively.

With an *asleep* planet, we function automatically, essentially driven by the demands of our environment and the habitual responses we adopted to cope with life at an earlier age.

With a *waking* planet, we are becoming aware of this automatic operation, perhaps long-established defensiveness, selfish ego-centred or even destructive behaviour. With this awareness we can begin to address and change our behaviour.

When a planet is *awake*, it is available to be used in full awareness by our higher self. It is no longer primarily used to satisfy personal egoistic desires, but to play our full part in our surroundings to the benefit of the greater whole.

On a re-reading of Chapter 6 you will be able to pick out instances of the planets operating at different levels. The following table gives example symptoms for each planet operating at the three levels: *asleep, waking, awake.*

Planet	'Asleep'	'Waking'	'Awake'
Mercury	Rote learning	Questioning	Clear communicator
Venus	Hedonist	Seeking harmony	Aesthetic
Mars	Aggressive	Harnessed action	Heroic
Jupiter	Sensualist	Develop judgement	Wise, just
Sun	Egotistic	Become self aware	Good will
Moon	Needy, childish	Losing defences	Open, childlike
Saturn	Habitual	Overcoming fears	Mature
Uranus	Rigid systems	Problem solving	Creative intelligence
Neptune	Fanatic	Develop conscience	Universal love
Pluto	Megalomania	Transformations	Spiritual will

Personality Integration

The psychological growth process involves the development of a balanced personality, where body, mind and feelings are co-operating and no one of them is unduly dominant.

Chapter 6 introduced the ego planets Sun, Moon and Saturn. As the *management team* of the personality/ ego, the ego planets have particular significance for its integration. The question is one of balance, and the expression or blocking of energies.

If there is an equitable balance between the ego planets, and the opportunity for each to express its energies according to its potential, then we are likely to have a balanced and integrated personality. If there are blocked energies, or undue dominance by one of these three fundamental aspects of the ego, then we are likely to have an unbalanced and non-integrated personality.

The propensity to these strengths and weaknesses is shown by various attributes we have already seen in the birth chart. Let us consider these, in order of importance.

- *Strength by house* (Chapter 8) is most important. The energies of an ego planet that is strongly positioned by house are likely to be in strong demand by the environment, and therefore easily expressed.
- *Strength by sign* (Chapter 7) is of next importance. The ego planet with the stronger inherent energies wanting to express themselves is likely to find easier expression if the environment is relatively neutral to either.
- Similarly, *a planet with a large number of aspects* to it is likely to find more outlets for its energies than one with few aspects.
- *Position of the ego planet in the chart* is also significant – Sun naturally finds its individual expression easier when it is high up in the chart; conversely Saturn prefers to be rooted in the collective near the bottom of the chart; and Moon is happiest near the horizon, involved in relationship with the world.
- Other qualitative factors such as the quality of aspects may also be relevant.

Assessing these factors can give an idea of which ego planet most easily expresses its energies, and which is likely to find it most difficult. Many people will find that simply *living* the strongest ego planet will automatically lead to integration of the weaker ones.

With Sun as the strongest ego planet, the key to integration is developing the will. With Moon, the key is contact, and understanding of emotional energies and feelings is most important. With Saturn, a pragmatic approach to life, attention to the physical body, and everyday practicalities are likely to be most important.

However, where there is significant imbalance and blockage, focus on the strongest ego planet may not be sufficient – specific attention may need to be given to developing the weakest ego planet.

Another factor to be considered is whether there are any aspects between the ego planets. As well as having significance in the Family Model (page 99), such aspects indicate where ego energies may flow with particular facility. This may lead to particularly well-entrenched sub-personalities, particularly in cases where all three ego planets are part of one aspect pattern. The person may feel integrated, as indeed they are in such a pattern – but they may be unaware of the character pattern involved, which may prove difficult to uncover.

Towards the Spiritual

Their generic name suggests that the transpersonal planets will have particular significance for establishing the link to the Higher Self.

Indeed, Uranus is described by Bruno and Louise Huber as *the Egg breaker*. This planet provides the transpersonal motivation together with the novelty of approach to pierce the shell of Assagioli's Egg and provide the impetus towards the spiritual, at some time during stage 3 of Andrew Harvey's growth journey. So times when the energies of Uranus are particularly activated by aspect to the Age Point are likely to be particularly propitious for sudden changes facilitating spiritual growth. Beware that these changes may not at the time be regarded as propitious by the ego, which will typically resist its own transcendence.

Neptune is the archetypal planet of spiritual love. We would thus expect Neptune to be important in the transition from the self-centredness of stage 2 to the other-centredness of the later parts of stage 3, and stage 4. As the mystics such as Rumi say, only through complete surrender to the divine love will we achieve the ultimate spiritual state.

Finally, Pluto is the archetypal planet of spiritual will, the planet of transformation and transcendence. This is the planet of ultimate change and transformation, of death and rebirth. It is through the energies of Pluto that the ego that developed at stage 2 is dissolved at stage 3, to bring alignment with the divine at stage 4.

Age Point in conjunction or opposition to any of the transpersonal planets is likely to indicate a time propitious for spiritual growth.

The Life Journey and the Life Clock

As we have seen in chapter 8, the houses help us to understand the challenges of the environment into which we were born and live. We can look at this as being the environment in which the soul has chosen to incarnate in order to learn the lessons it needs this time around.

Uncovering conflicts between nature and nurture (Chapter 9) is likely to be of particular significance for the individual's psychological growth. The adaptations of childhood can prove particularly deep-rooted blockers to our development.

In Chapter 10 we saw how the progression of the Age Point through the houses, and around the Life Clock, shows the generic life stages through which we all pass. Various chart features are highlighted as the Age Point progresses around the Life Clock, making aspects to planets and stimulating the corresponding aspect patterns. This shines a spotlight onto particular areas of our lives, and aspects of our psyche. These represent the opportunity to uncover previous limitations and desirable directions, and to make the changes necessary for our growth.

The passing of Age Point through the Low Points of the houses is of particular spiritual significance. The Low Point is the closest point to the centre of the chart, symbolising our spiritual centre. So at these times of life we can most easily contact the energies of our true selves, and the ideas that relate to our true purpose in this lifetime.

Other Spiritual Indicators

There are two further objects that are of particular astrological and spiritual significance, but do not correspond with real physical objects in the solar system – the Moon's North Node and the ascendant.

The Moon's North Node   ☊

The Moon's North Node is not a planet, and does not correspond with any physical object in the solar system. Technically, it corresponds with the point of intersection of the Moon's orbit with the plane of the ecliptic. This is of no great interest here, and we will concentrate on its symbolic meaning.

Of course there must be two points of intersection of these orbits, and the other one is known as the Moon's South Node (☋). This does not appear on the Huber birth chart; if it did, it would be positioned exactly opposite the North Node.

The North Node has been found to represent such a significant focal point that it appears on the birth chart with similar status to planets, receiving aspects in a similar way.

The Hubers describe the North Node as being rather like a compass needle in its ability to find the right way to improve our character. If we are going through periods of confusion in life, the Node and its house positioning give the direction of the way ahead. In a sense, the meaning of the occupied house is the meaning of the Node, and this house will usually provide the right source for the next step that is important for this individual.

This will generally not be easy. It is usually in the opposite house, that of the South Node, that we find it most comfortable to be and where our habits lead us. The North Node is taking us out of our comfort zone towards what will best challenge us in order to grow.

For example, with North Node in the 12th house, we may find it very easy to spend all our waking hours serving others in the 6th house, not finding the time to be on our own, go within and develop the inner resources that at heart we really need.

Any planets that are in aspect to the North Node are likely to provide effective tools to help initiate the action needed to move towards it.

Periods of life when the Age Point comes into conjunction or opposition with the North Node, or with these planets, are likely to be of particular significance.

The Ascendant Sign

The other significant point of intersection in the birth chart is that between the signs and the houses, between the zodiac and the horizon at birth – at the ascendant (AC) and descendant (DC).

The ascendant represents the point where the zodiac is coming up over the eastern horizon at the time of birth – so the ascendant sign is also sometimes referred to as the *Rising Sign*. This sign, the birth point in terms of the Life Clock, is said to be of particular spiritual significance, representing the inner goal of our lives. We grow towards the qualities of the ascendant sign (the spiritual journey is essentially about the development of qualities and character, not about material circumstances.)

Although this gives a guiding light, it does not necessarily provide much of a practical pointer. The North Node points more practically to where we should seek to take the next step towards that goal.

Planets positioned on or close to the AC or DC are similarly likely to have particular spiritual significance.

Summary – Psychological and Spiritual Growth

- Theories of reincarnation and karma are consistent with the approach of astrological psychology.

- The signs of the zodiac symbolise the soul's journey of incarnation and development.

- There is a four-stage model for psychological and spiritual growth of the individual: from childhood, through ego-domination, to psychological and spiritual development, and to enlightenment. Earlier chapters were all concerned in different ways with helping this growth process.

- The planets operate at different levels, asleep, waking and awake. With increasing self awareness we can begin to raise their levels of operation.

- Integration of the ego planets is a key to psychological development.

- The transpersonal planets relate to key stages of the spiritual development process.

- The ascendant sign and the North Node are of particular significance, identifying respectively the spiritual goal and the next step.

- Planets positioned on the AC/DC, and those in aspect to the North Node, have related significance.

12. Bringing It All Together

"No astrologer - and as well no psychoanalyst - can interpret a life and destiny at a level higher than that at which he himself functions."

Dane Rudhyar

In this final chapter we bring together what has gone before and demonstrate how some of the techniques outlined can be used practically in chart interpretation. The art of interpretation is a combination of technical know-how and intuitive inspiration, based on a sound understanding of the psychological approach developed by Bruno and Louise Huber.

This needs to be accompanied by considerable personal experience of working with the charts of real people rather than charts of celebrities and historical figures, who are not going to be on hand to offer feedback or discuss their charts. Real people can give immediate feedback; they can share specific details of their life experience which may be sparked off by a comment or suggestion put forward by the astrologer.

Channels of communication are opened up through dialogue between astrologer and client so that deep exploration and deep healing can take place; the astrological session becomes a sacred space. The professional astrologer who works with people in this way will require additional training in counselling in order to serve the client, and the issues that arise during the session, in a clear and centred way.

Technical and Intuitive Approaches

The technical information in this book offers an overview of the main features of astrological psychology which can be used in chart interpretation. These techniques give guidelines, not rules, and can be used as a framework on which to base the interpretation. The astrologer needs a certain amount of technical understanding to enable them to organise and structure the information and details in the chart, which should be considered alongside the intuitive response that the chart evokes.

Technical and intuitive approaches merge and blend in the art of interpretation. The astrologer gains an overall feel for the chart, using the eyes and senses; an aesthetic impression of the chart's appearance can be made and it is likely that the eye will be drawn to one particular feature. Some charts look distinctive, others less so, but all will have features which stand out. What first draws the eye and the intuition is then backed up and supported by the astrologer's technical knowledge and understanding.

Bruno Huber
29.11.1930, 11:55 Zürich, CH

Taking first the intuitive approach, look at the chart above using your eyes and senses, and leaving aside any technical know-how you have, consider the following:

What do you notice first?

What jumps out at you?

What for you are the most striking features in the chart?

What are your immediate reactions to the chart?

Perhaps jot down a few words.

What does your intuition tell you a) about the chart, and b) about the person whose chart it is?

Now let's take a more technical approach, using a few of the features covered in this book in the early chapters, and consider:

The visual image in the chart.

The overall chart shaping and its associated motivation.

The direction the aspect structure is moving in.

The orientation of the aspect structure.

Are there any open spaces in the chart?

It may already have become obvious, when looking at the chart as a whole, that the technical and intuitive approaches flow into and complement each other. With practice it can become difficult to just look at a chart and not allow a visual image to emerge.

Using the senses and intuition as we look at this chart, we may be struck by its strong, upward-reaching appearance. This may be the chart of someone who has high aspirations, who seeks to move upwards in their own individuation process. Blending this with the technical know-how we already have of the chart image, we may see mountains in the overall chart structure, and a series of mountain peaks reaching across the top of the chart. These spring from a pyramid shape which gives a broad and solid base to the image in the central area of the chart.

The shaping of the aspect structure as a whole suggests a combination of fixed motivation (the four-sided *pyramid* figure) and mutable motivation (the large triangular shapes). The triangular shapes dominate and stand out, suggesting more emphasis on mutability than fixity. There is a feeling of quivering, actively sensitive movement in this chart, with the mountain peaks at the top hinting at different focal points of interest, ambition, achievement and heights to be scaled, yet always moving upwards from the solid base across in the lower half of the chart.

This is the chart of Bruno Huber and as well as reflecting the essence of the man, the mountain peaks are reminiscent of his native Switzerland. Bruno was no stranger to the mountains as he often went skiing or cycling in them. And his life's work involved intense empirical research into human potential, problems of the human psyche and of the psychological-spiritual development of the individual, using the unique blend of astrology and psychosynthesis which became known as astrological psychology or the Huber Method.

Checklist of Main Chart Features

When beginning to interpret a chart it is helpful to bear in mind what you are looking for. Interpretation requires preparation. Of course it is possible with experience to look at a chart informally and make some off the cuff comments, but when approaching a one-to-one session with someone, whether they be family, friend, or the fee-paying client, it is important for the astrologer to allow time beforehand to centre themselves quietly and focus on the chart they will be looking at.

The following checklist of points to consider is a helpful aid in this process. It includes all the main points to consider, which have been outlined in this book. The list might seem long and daunting, but with practice and experience it is possible to cover all these points... and more.

Chart Interpretation Checklist

Connect with the centre and focus yourself.

Look at the chart – use your eyes and senses. Is there an intuitive image or picture? What does this say?

Consider the shaping/motivation.

Look at the balance of colour.

What direction is the chart moving in – vertical/ horizontal?

Which hemispheres are emphasised, containing more planets?

Which quadrants are emphasised?

Are there recognisable aspect patterns?

Are any planets blocked off? Unaspected? Intercepted?

Are there Cuspal, Low Point or Stressed planets?

Assess the strength of the planets by sign and house.

Is there any major polarity in the chart, suggesting conflict?

What is the comparative strength of the ego planets?

What does the Family Model suggest?

Consider the house/area of life of the Moon's North Node.

Look at the current movement of Age Point in the Life Clock.

Perhaps most important is the first point. The circle at the centre of the chart represents the clear space within the person whose chart is being interpreted. The interpretation begins here as we connect with and acknowledge the essential divinity within ourselves and our client; we meet on equal ground, in an equal space that is free of judgement and full of unconditional love and acceptance.

Bringing it Together – Examples

Now we give two example chart interpretations which bring together the approaches covered in this book. In the first example there was ongoing discussion with the client about her chart, much as there would be in a live consultation.

Example 1 – Georgina

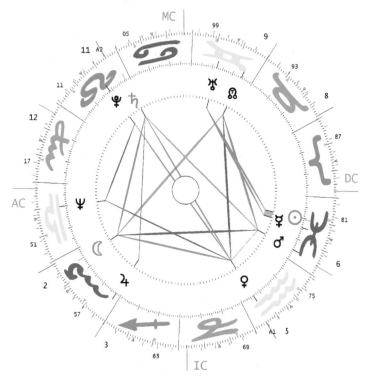

Georgina
10.03.1947, 19:10 Leeds, England

Georgina is an attractive and youthful woman in her late 50's at the time of this consultation (2004). She is an only child, is married with two grown-up sons, has taken early retirement from teaching and is enjoying pursuing a variety of new artistic and keep fit activities as well as having regular contact with her elderly mother who lives 25 miles distant.

One image that can be seen in her chart is of a large container with firm sides. This sits centrally in the chart, with its open top facing the MC. There is an impression of lots of activity going on around this central container, perhaps distracting her attention. The overall appearance is of her wanting to stand firm, to be a solid presence, yet with plenty going on around her.

Georgina speaks of needing to have structure in her life, but rather than feeling her attention might be distracted by what appears to be external activity, she says she goes actively looking for things to do, and for people to meet. She is happy to initiate things.

The overall shaping of the chart is fixed – there are quadrangular figures – and this suggests that she is motivated towards security, stability and preserving and maintaining a sense of status quo in her life. The whole chart structure has a vertical feel, indicating that she could be ambitious, but her Sun is close to the Low Point in the 6th house, indicating that it may have been difficult for her to assert herself, and have a sense of her own self-confidence, particularly in the workplace.

Georgina acknowledges this and says that when she was working, she was the one who felt this, so she put pressure on herself to be ultra-efficient. The pressure came from within, and she speaks of having high expectations of herself and the need to be perfect. Now that she has retired, that pressure is gone.

There are several horizontal aspects in the chart, drawing her towards contact and communication with others. There is quite a strong pull into the 2nd quadrant of the chart, reinforcing her need for contact and fitting in with society and the world around her, together with an easy ability to do so.

The balance of aspect colours in Georgina's chart is 6 red, 3 green and 5 blue. There is an excess of red *doing* energy available to her and this is reflected by the Efficiency Triangle present in the aspect structure. She readily agrees that she becomes very actively involved in any project or undertaking she commits to, and wants to give of her best, often aiming for 110% in perfection and getting things right. She says she is not a risk taker, so to ensure things are absolutely right she will put in a lot of research beforehand, drawing on the excess red her chart contains. It may, however, be useful for her to note this and be aware, using the green aspects, that with a high red quotient and slightly less blue, she could get carried away to the point of exhaustion if she does not build in rest time and allow for recuperation and a recharge of the batteries.

The Efficiency Triangle has Saturn and Venus at the ends of the opposition aspect with Moon at the apex. Moon and Venus together in this pattern suggest a focus on relationship and emotional contacts, but Saturn may well be something of a stickler for getting things right in this particular area of life, and for keeping any emotional outpourings under control. For Georgina, this will not necessarily be uncomfortable. Her Moon, the apex planet and therefore the outlet source of the energy embedded in this pattern, is in Scorpio, so keeping her deep feelings more guarded is something she will do naturally. Yet when she does express how she feels, it will be total and heartfelt and she is likely to get a strong sense of personal satisfaction from caring for others – and of being appreciated and taken care of herself.

It is notable that five planets are in water signs – Moon, Jupiter, Sun, Mercury, Mars. With three of them in sensitive and compassionate Pisces, she will have a strong inner emotional and caring nature. Georgina acknowledges this in herself, and says she can quite easily be moved to tears – again, Saturn's role here could be significant as a protector.

Looking at a couple of the other aspect patterns in her chart, we will see that she also has a Single Ambivalence figure (Venus, Pluto, Neptune), with Neptune as the *escape* planet where the two blue aspects meet. Neptune is in the 1st house of the chart, where she will want to enjoy, celebrate and experience doing her own thing.

Georgina's interest in art and music since she took early retirement is something that she gains pleasure and a sense of inner peace from. She has reconnected with her voice and her ability to sing, something she had not done for many years, and she joined a singing group in 2000, soon after she retired. Away from the tensions of work in an inner city high school which, when she was working, could have been experienced in the opposition aspect of this pattern, she is now able to explore the creative potential and the greater sense of just *being* that Neptune can offer. She has reconnected with her own spiritual path and has returned to attending church fairly regularly. She calls this her oasis and quiet time which nourishes and nurtures her inner space, which is something she feels she needs.

Georgina has a Microscope aspect pattern in her chart which has not been outlined in this book. Its lens is focussed on the 2nd quadrant of the chart, pointing directly towards the 5th house. The Microscope has fixed shaping and motivation, with all three aspect colours present, and is able to make

Microscope

detailed and precise observations on the area of life on which the lens is focussed.

Relationships and friendships play a central role in Georgina's life. She is good at keeping in touch with friends and acquaintances, extending the circle of those she knows to younger people as well as those of her own age. She admits to being something of an oracle when it comes to knowing how her friends and contacts are faring and what is going on in their lives. Venus in Aquarius, strongly placed on the 5th house cusp and part of the Microscope, reinforces the importance of relationships in her life, and her easy ability to socialise.

Saturn, which is opposite Venus, might come on strong, sometimes bringing more control and restraint to this and other areas of life than is appropriate. But Saturn is weak by sign, is stressed before the 11th house cusp and is visually quite dominant in her chart. Being high in the chart it seems almost to hold up several aspect patterns. With Saturn in this position, she could feel that she has quite a lot to live up to, with she herself being the most demanding task-master of all.

Georgina readily confesses to being capable of putting a lot of pressure on herself, and of being a perfectionist. This was especially true whilst she was working as a special needs coordinator, heading a team and chairing policy meetings. Her Efficiency Triangle, with stressed Saturn as one of the pinning planets, was the major driving force in her life; there wasn't room or time for much else, and her weakly-placed Sun, close to the Low Point in the 6th house and the closest planet to the DC, was constantly under pressure from within to assert itself and perform in the workplace.

Georgina enjoyed teaching until she became a special needs coordinator later in her career. Prior to this she had taught for several years after her marriage in 1970, which took place as her Age Point (AP) was approaching conjunction with Venus and opposition with Saturn. She says that at that time, getting married was viewed as a way of conforming, and for her it was also a means of gaining greater security. She has a good marriage and a supportive husband. They met just before her 18th birthday, shortly after her AP entered Capricorn, reinforcing the needed backdrop of stability and security that was around for her at this particular time in her life, when she left home to attend a teacher training college in the south.

Georgina's eldest son was born when she was on the Low Point of the 5th house, and her second son when her AP was conjunct Mars. This period of time spans the lens of the Microscope figure and she relates this to a time of being immersed in the social *mother and baby* scene; she is still in touch with friends she made during this period.

She speaks of the period of life between ages 33 and 34 as being very difficult. Her grandmother, who had lived in the family home with her parents, died. Georgina had grown up with her, was close to her and adored her, and it is interesting to note that Uranus, which can represent the grandmother, is the highest planet in the chart. Soon after this her father became ill with cancer and died the following year. Georgina was very close to him and the pain of his illness and loss was deep. Her AP at this time was in Pisces, reflecting the emotional backdrop of her life and the intensity of her feelings. The AP was also on the 6th house Low Point and was making a conjunction to the Sun, the planet which represents the father in the Family Model.

Georgina returned to teaching in 1984, after her AP had moved from Pisces to Aries, and had crossed the DC at age 36. She tells of how, at this stage her self-esteem was high. She felt energised, youthful and empowered. New horizons were opening up, and she gradually took on more responsibilities in the school where she worked.

But had she sometimes felt as if she was at a loss, *all at sea*, with some of the things she was undertaking in her career? Her AP at this time was opposite Neptune – suggesting that, when teaching, there might have been times when it felt like she was on stage without knowing all her lines. Georgina confirms this experience, describing the subjects she was asked to teach, which have strong Neptunian qualities. One of them was art, which was not the main subject she had trained in. She felt slightly out of her depth in a subject area that was less familiar, but her Efficiency Triangle swung into action and she immersed herself in all the aspects of art she needed to understand, from technique to art history. She was also required to teach photography, with which she was unfamiliar, yet she undertook this challenge willingly, learning to use the school's dark room and the techniques of developing and printing.

Viewing Saturn as the ego planet which signifies the way Georgina gains a sense of herself physically, its stressed position becomes significant. In the mid 1990's her health was seriously undermined by the stresses of the job. By this stage of her career she had moved into the area of special needs. Initially enjoying this aspect of teaching, she had been appointed special needs coordinator for the school where she taught.

In 1995, soon after the AP had changed signs, had moved into the 9th house and was conjunct the Moon's North Node, she discovered she had breast cancer, opted for immediate surgery, a mastectomy. Her treatment and recovery were an example of courage and positive thinking. She took extended sick leave and returned to teaching the following year, but found that the stresses of the job and the expectations put upon her were too challenging. She says "special needs grew out of hand", the demands of her role becoming overburdened by legislation.

Georgina became ill again when her AP was conjunct Uranus. This time her illness was not life threatening, but it was unexpected and uncomfortable (irritable bowel syndrome). She was under stress again, reflecting the stressed position of Saturn in the Efficiency Triangle, and knew she had to make big changes in her life. Georgina went on sick leave again, and this time decided not to return to teaching. She took early retirement in 2000, just as her AP moved into Cancer.

She returned to being at home and reconnecting with domestic life, embracing this with pleasure, becoming interested once again in cooking, gardening, socialising with friends. With the experience of illness behind her she looked for ways to nurture and care for her body. Aerobics, yoga, swimming, walking and eating wisely are all now part of her regime. Saturn is much more at ease, and so is she.

In the Family Model we see that Saturn, symbolising the mothering principle, is higher in the chart than Sun and Moon. This suggests that she may have seen her mother as being the most important member of the family grouping. However, Georgina didn't see her mother as the one who pulled the strings or had the final word. Her mother did not go out to work and was always there for her (along with her grandmother – Uranus high in the chart), and with this set up we might expect to find Saturn in the lower rather than the upper hemisphere of the chart.

Georgina speaks of her father, symbolised by the Sun and in a separate linear aspect, with great affection. Even though her mother managed the household, she says that her father's word was final, especially if she'd done anything wrong. This shows how important it is to discuss with a client their own experience and memory; simply applying the guidelines and assuming we've got it right doesn't always work.

Georgina says that if she argued with a parent when she was younger, it would have been her mother. She speaks of standing up to her; the square aspect between Moon and Saturn reflects the likelihood of this kind of interaction. As an adult she is now very close to her mother.

Example 2 – Lucy

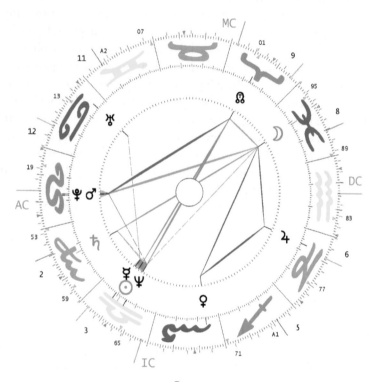

Lucy
05.10.1949, 02:00 Liverpool, England

Our second example is presented differently. It was undertaken as an exercise in interpretation by the astrologer, who made notes on the initial assessment of Lucy's chart before seeing her. This was then presented to her for feedback and comments. Her very honest comments are shown in italics and have been inserted into the relevant part of the text, which thus appears in the form of a dialogue.

Bear in mind that there is no way that astrology can give the precise details of a person's life – we are all different. But it can lay the foundations for a trusting relationship between client and counsellor so that the former is encouraged to enter into the relationship with openness and honesty, two essential qualities if the client is wanting to move forward in their life.

Astrologer: When I first look at Lucy's chart I am aware of two almost separated patterns, a passive all blue triangle and a far more active, mainly red and green structure. The intuitive image I get is of a balancing act where the blue figure is striving to hold up the more dominant structure on the tip of one finger (the Moon) – fearful lest it be overwhelmed should it collapse. This suggests to me that there are two main areas of Lucy's personality – one peaceful, harmonious, happy and caring, and the other a far more dynamic and actively creative part.

Lucy: All of my life I have had a conflict going on between two selves. The part of me that has tended to predominate throughout my life is the part that wants, needs, seeks and makes compromises for harmony, balance and peace. I genuinely love others to be happy and do enjoy helping to bring this about.

For years I was too keen to do anything for a quiet life – which resulted in neglecting my own needs and myself. In retrospect I recognise that this behaviour created underlying resentment, self-pity and a victim mentality. I didn't acknowledge the extent of the inner conflict until later years. I suppressed the inner drive and sense of personal power inside me, as I was afraid of it, not knowing how to manage its outward manifestation. I was painfully shy in relationships and very vulnerable to criticism until my mid-20s. I remember being called an exhibitionist during a rare display of exuberance at the office, aged about 20, after which I was careful not to express too much joy!

Throughout my life, when I've been moved to do something that seemed impossible and I've really made up my mind, then nothing will stop me. I can then feel insuperable, and excel. Something clicks inside me, and there is no going back. There is a part of me that would love to be lazy, and be free to dream, but I've never had much space to give in to the laziness, as it's been quite a driven life. A new friend said recently "you look so ordinary, but you are extraordinary". He said he meant that in outward appearance I can seem like a quiet mouse, but then there are those times when – shockingly – the inner lioness appears. I've sometimes been likened to a frightened rabbit or Cinderella, but I do feel that in recent years the victim sign has disappeared from my forehead. In September 1998, a series of synchronistic occurrences led me to the path of self-empowerment. I think the more the dynamic aspects of my personality have been expressed more in recent years. It now feels like the dynamic me and the quiet me have joined in the dance together, in harmony.

Astrologer: Since the dynamic and creative part of her can be a stressful area it is possible that she may feel happier living a quieter and more peaceful existence in the blue rather than acknowledging and making use of the real power of the more active figure, although when needs must, such as ensuring survival, e.g. paying the bills, she will access this energy to create and do.

Lucy: Now at almost 55 it is absolutely true that I am finding incredible strength post divorce etc., to survive, pay the bills and finance education for a daughter and training for myself. I'm working very hard for a number of years at something I don't really enjoy, looking forward to reaching another turning point at age 56. I've let go of the earlier, dominating fear that I "might not have enough" and embraced the concept of abundance in my life, which doesn't just mean money.

Astrologer: I note that the passive figure – a Small Talent Triangle – is spanning the right (or 'You') side of the chart and the more dynamic, active figure mainly inhabits the left (or 'I') side of the chart. Although dynamic because of its red and green nature, it is a quadrilateral figure and will therefore use its energy to achieve security in one form or another. The linking planet is the Moon, situated in 8th house Pisces. With three green aspects to it, it is sensitive and potentially vulnerable…

Lucy: I've been emotionally very vulnerable, always finding it difficult to express my true feelings and needs. I remember spending much of my life not really knowing what I wanted, not understanding my own feelings and the pain they caused. I gave way too easily to the will of others (though this is no longer the case), as the people around me always seemed to know what they wanted and I got positive feedback from pleasing others. Early parental influences were quite strict and Victorian. Self-assertion was interpreted as selfish, and somehow unbecoming.

Astrologer: …but the Moon is probably able to function at an intuitive level…

Lucy: I am very intuitive, but this has often been more useful to me at work, where I've always acted on the instant "knowing" about people and situations. Earlier in my personal/emotional life, I would sometimes override my intuition. More than anything, I suppose I tended to adapt to others wishes, in order to please.

Astrologer: ...and will know when it is the right time to choose to be in the blue and chill out, or perhaps keep the peace, depending on circumstances, and when there is the need to be more active and assertive. Although the blue figure appears passive, blue is to do with security and in this context Venus in Scorpio may indicate hidden under-currents of possessiveness or envy.

Lucy: I experienced incredible feelings of envy as a child – mostly about other girls who seemed to be doted on by their parents, and received lots of attention from them. I envied the pretty presents they received, big time. There was one particular girl, an only child, always talking about lovely family things and bringing in presents. Hard to admit it, but my jealousy/ envy was so intense, I sometimes imagined having a knife and... !

No emotions are as strong as a kid's troubled emotions. I think by the time I was more grown up, life and I had done a great job of convincing me that I wasn't worthy anyway, and nice things like expressions of love and affection were for others. From 26 I had this love in bundles from my Mum and through my children. I'd never doubted my Dad's great love, but it was more passive. Even now I would love to experience admiring, romantic love from the first time expressions of a partner, but will be OK without it if that is the way it goes.

Possessiveness? – this was squeezed out by my sense of unworthiness. I got used to not being my husband's first and foremost. I do admit to having been possessive about my two daughters, but feel I've mastered it... don't even mind them being with the 'other woman' now!

Astrologer: So when meeting Lucy for the first time which part of her will we encounter? Whether we are met by the passive, cheerful blue Lucy or the active red and green Lucy is likely to depend on whether we meet her socially or in a working situation.

With Pluto/Mars on the AC, even with no red aspects to this pair, Lucy has the ability to be a strong and powerful person, but to what extent does she use this? Far too often girls are brought up with negative messages about being strong willed and assertive, so they grow into adulthood with this part of themselves suppressed.

Lucy: From early childhood, through teens, my mother was a very powerful influence. She absolutely did not approve of my strong will and assertiveness when it popped out. I felt repressed and thoroughly disapproved of. At around two years old, I went through a phase of biting people. My childhood was suffused with the feeling of being unliked and unlikeable, being squashed and repressed, and the overpowering weight of unfairness. I was miserably unhappy much of the time, and remember feeling unloved. I did naughty things, presumably because I was unhappy and seeking attention, and then got punished for the results of being so unhappy – leading to greater unhappiness and an even greater sense of unfairness. This didn't seem to be happening to my darling oldest sister, the tougher second one – nor the sweet angel baby who arrived when I was five, of whom I was intensely jealous for years. There was a lot of teasing and bullying from the two older sisters, one of whom still remarks from time to time that it's a wonder I'm normal.

Astrologer: And in this case Lucy also has Saturn (mother) opposite Moon (child). This suggests that the more restrictive messages might have been quite strong. In any case, for Lucy, security and maintaining the status quo will always tend to be important.

Lucy: I've always felt really uncomfortable with conflict and would instinctively feel it was my responsibility to get the boat back on an even keel if loved ones were upset. I've never been able to say things to people that would hurt, under any circumstances. To deal with conflict, I'd slip into calm and passive mode, and especially through school years would retreat into myself. I wasn't very successful with friendships then, probably because I lacked self-belief. Throughout a difficult marriage, I switched to rational discussion as a (rather inadequate) means of conflict resolution.

Astrologer: Quite apart from being strongly Libran with a need to achieve a balance in relationship situations, she has Saturn, with red and green aspects, just into the 2nd house and opposition Moon suggesting the likelihood that emotional fears will sometimes inhibit action. But, as we shall see, Saturn isn't always negative.

The dominant figure consists of two Irritation Triangles, a Search Triangle and a single Ambivalence Triangle. This is where the work gets done and when Lucy applies herself to a task it will be done with authority and with Leo cheerfulness and determination (Mars/Pluto). She is able to plan carefully (Saturn in Virgo), use creative imagination (Sun/Neptune/Mercury in Libra in square aspect to Uranus), and finally bring compassion (Moon in Pisces on the 'You' side of the chart) in to her interactions with others.

But I get the feeling that this area of Lucy's personality could be a bit of a whirlwind and that she will feel the need to take time out from this very sensitive and demanding structure. The Pluto/Mars conjunction in the 1st house can be self-protective, especially in a situation where Lucy's feelings are hurt or when she is stressed, so she probably knows when to stop and go back into the blue.

Lucy: I worked at the Civil Service from 18-25 and was poached for a key job at Regional Office at the age of 23. Had my own office where all the personal files for the Staff of the Region were kept, and the keys. I saw my own staff reports, and was considered to be an all-rounder – learned quickly, fast, was personable, communicative, outgoing, discreet, had the drive to organise, and the sensitivity to deal with staff issues. The lost mark on my report was because "Lucy can tend to cavil" – exactness can sometimes be criticism or carping! Whilst being given the opportunity to work and fire on all cylinders (and I adored the recognition) I did at the same time demand perfection of myself, and from time to time would feel exhausted. This remains a pattern, and I reach the point a couple of times a year when it matters not what might still need to be done – I need a weekend of sleep therapy, and crash.

Astrologer: With Sun, Mercury, Neptune and the South Node in the 3rd house (mutable air) and in Libra (cardinal air) I would expect that Lucy will have more than her fair share of intelligence and learning ability, will have done well at school and most likely have a natural flair for languages.

Lucy: From starting French age 11, I found that languages were my thing. I learned French almost by absorption, loved the grammar, it was pleasure not work. Learnt German fluently and I speak a little Dutch.

Astrologer: With a vertical chart she will want to make something of her talents in this direction and will want to be seen by others to have achieved. Moon is the highest of the ego planets which suggests that as a child she may have felt that she had to take responsibility for her own direction in life and that there was no role model to follow.

But will the opposition to Moon have been a help or a hindrance to her succeeding? Moon opposition Saturn suggests there was some conflict between mother and daughter and whilst she may have had a mother who was caring and protective but who didn't encourage her to go out into the world and find out what she could do to be successful, she may equally have had a mother who wanted her to make something of herself and supported her from behind.

Lucy: My Mum really was a caring and loving person, even though I didn't feel loved in my childhood and teens. I used to feel that she didn't understand me, and even that she didn't really like me. (We later discovered each other as soul-mates and shared the most wonderful mother-daughter relationship when I was around 24/25 until her death when I was 41.) She was absent a lot from home from the time I was 11 years old, as she worked evenings. I felt lost, directionless and powerless during childhood.

I was offered a place at Liverpool University to take French, but was terrified of the big world, especially of trying to overcome my acute shyness to try to make friends. I was afraid of not being liked, of rejection. I found it difficult to articulate my feelings, and felt sick at the thought of charting my course through those turbulent studenty waters. So I got married ("security", to someone 11 years older) at 18, instead of going to University.

Astrologer: The Moon in the 8th house suggests that Lucy would get emotional satisfaction, as well as security from working in the public sector, either in a profession or perhaps in local government or other community organisation.

Lucy: I did work in the public sector, and liked the fact that it felt secure and safe. Whilst doing a temporary job at Littlewoods before taking up the first Civil Service job at age 18, I was offered the job of a buyer at Littlewoods. There was a frisson at doing something so creative and unstructured – travelling etc. My new husband didn't like the sound of that, and I bowed to his wishes – and then there was that security of the civil service job... However, I didn't really like the stuffy, confined feeling of the regular hours, and am again, later in life, poised to break free of that straitjacket structure.

Astrologer: Age Progression suggests that at age 18 Lucy was still intent on developing her intellectual talents, but then the AP falls into intercepted Scorpio so perhaps her intentions were thwarted. Or perhaps, because the AP makes no further contact with the active *doing* aspect structure until later in life, she went the way of someone else.

She was entering a passive *blue* period, perhaps devoted to having children during the period when AP was between Venus and Jupiter, especially since AP would have been opposite creative Uranus in 1976.

Lucy: In 1976 I had my first daughter (second one in 1979). I was euphoric in motherhood, and the high lasted for years. Raising children felt creative, successful, beautiful, worthwhile... everything that was good, albeit exhausting. I enjoyed these years of my life hugely, and felt fortunate that I could be a full-time mother and home-maker.

Astrologer: When Lucy was coming up to 36 and on the 7th house cusp her AP would have been opposite Mars/Pluto. Possibly this signified a time when she became aware of the need to rediscover her *doing* self. Or perhaps, since she was entering the 7th house, it signified the start of changes in her relationships which may then have gone through an unstable phase as AP progressed through the sign of Pisces.

Lucy: At age 33-34 my world fell apart. My marriage was in serious trouble, and the betrayal by the "other woman", whom I knew well, made the situation doubly painful. I saw myself as a nothing, a shattered vase, with no form left. I felt annihilated as a person. I recognised it would be a slow process to re-build myself painfully, piece by piece, and had a sense that the reconstructed me would have a different form.

I entered a long period, years of self-searching. I felt that most of what I had ever believed in or thought in terms of relationships and emotions had all been illusion, and it was time to reconstruct a new reality on my own terms, by thinking, reflecting. The old ideas were of no use, no help. This seemed totally negative and depressing then, but it was actually the beginning of a slow metamorphosis, the start of a new way of being me – if I could only survive the agony of that first phase. I did. A new personal mantra emerged from somewhere: "my day will come". I don't know where this came from, but it was my light at the end of the tunnel. The next years were a long and very determined process of self-development.

Astrologer: However, at the age of 42/43 she would have made a direct connection with her own aspect pattern again (Moon) and whilst Saturn and security needs may have inhibited her from making any immediate move, this was the time when she was able to get in touch with her own power house and maybe make important decisions for her own future.

Important changes would have culminated in 2000 and 2001 when AP opposed those planets, including Sun – her own sense of self, in the 3rd house and conjoined the North Node in the 9th house, pointing the way ahead.

Lucy: Age 36 I decided to start an Open University degree so that I could become self-reliant, and earn a living for myself in the future. By age 44 (1993) I had a BA Hons. in Politics. I then started work (first time since 1974) for an International association, for which I still work.

Probably the toughest decision I have ever made came in 1999 when, still full of fear but with total resolve, I left the marital home and all its security and started divorce proceedings which were contentious and culminated in divorce in June 2001. 2000/2001 was an intense and very focused period of spiritual development, which helped me deal with the emotional turbulence. I spent a weekend per month for 2 years immersed in Taoist teachings and tai chi, and found the simple and profound principles transforming and liberating. I emerged from this with much peace in my heart, for the first time in my life. The relationship with my ex-husband has also transformed and we are, unexpectedly, kindly friends. I still live alone, but am not lonely, nor needy. If and when a new partner does come along, my long-time-waiting romantic self is ready..!

Astrologer: This chart shows an integration of the three ego planets involved in the Family Model, Sun, Saturn and Moon. In fact the integration is achieved only through the conjunction of Sun with Neptune so does this indicate a very loving relationship between child and parents, or does it suggest that there was some confusion?

Lucy: The relationship with my mother went from very difficult to being very close by age of 24/25. My father was always a steady, loving, kind, strong, secure presence in the home. He would often reminisce about the war, so everyone tried to avoid getting caught by the stories, which could last forever. I couldn't bear to hurt his feelings by sidling away, so became a good listener. He would say of me 'our Lucy is a brick', as I often helped him with jobs in the house, like wallpapering, and unfreezing pipes in the loft in the winter. I received praise for being reliable, tenacious, and utterly dependable. And indeed, I wanted to be, especially for my Dad. He was the best. Autonomy and assertiveness were not in my vocabulary until around 36 – then part of the reason for starting the OU course was because my husband didn't want me to do it!!

Astrologer: In any case, Lucy will have grown up with strong parental ties that would have made it more likely for her to initially choose the passive rather than the assertive role in life. There is often a sense of obligation or guilt with such a pattern, which can inhibit the child from feeling free to break the emotional ties and achieve autonomy. The Sun in the *collective* hemisphere may also have made it less easy for Lucy to see the way ahead and unleash the power of her assertive self.

What about Lucy today? At the time of writing (August 2004) she is just coming up to age 55 so her AP will have crossed the MC and will once again be in a *blue* area of the chart. She is likely to have gone though dramatic and emotional changes during the past 12 years so that now she has a much better sense of the purpose. In a counselling session she may feel there is a need to clarify where she is now and to have confirmation that all that may have changed in her life was truly meant to have done so.

Issues to be looked at might be whether Lucy found a balance on the Nodal axis so that she can not only expand her thinking but find ways of bringing knowledge and understanding to others? And whether she has an understanding of the esoteric meaning of the ascending sign of Leo...

Her AP is now in the *being* quadrant and once again intercepted, in the creative sign of Taurus, so maybe these next few years are a time for inner reflection and the development of new skills, or perhaps the developing or deepening of spiritual values.

Lucy: Looking back at my life, I see I've made an incredible journey, and have found my self. I'm retraining in life-coaching/NLP/counselling, which combine and overlap with the spiritual training which is still central to my life. I have a huge desire to help others move forward out of stuck places, discover more about themselves, live their values and create their own reality. I do at times make excuses to myself about "taking that leap" from the job I am so familiar with, into uncharted territory. But I am on course, curious, open, and ready for the next changes when they happen.

Reflection

The examples are of two very different people, with different charts and life experiences, yet both Georgina and Lucy shared difficulties and challenges in their lives at ages 33 – 34, when they were moving through the Low Point of the 6th house, and again when the AP went over the DC and new areas of opportunity opened up for them both.

In the Chapter 10 it was pointed out that Age Progression is a simple, clear and straightforward technique giving valuable results. Whilst it is not suggested that these two examples offer proof of this, it is interesting to see how, in the charts of two real people chosen by two different astrological counsellors, the experiences each of the subjects had at these ages were noted by them both as being of significance – showing clearly how this relates to their Age Progression.

What Next?

This book gives an overview of how astrological psychology works and how it can be applied and used as a tool to further personal and spiritual growth. This provides a relatively simple outline of techniques which ultimately need to be considered in much greater depth.

Further study is necessary for students to go deeper into the wealth of insights astrological psychology can offer, to understand the theory of the psychological motivations that can be found in the birth chart in a manner that encourages the individual to develop greater self-awareness.

There are also more advanced techniques, offering deeper insights, that we have not covered at all. For example, the Moon Node Chart gives insights into karma and the shadow personality. The House Chart shows how the environment shaped and conditioned us during our formative years, so can reveal conditioned behaviour.

If the ideas in this book have whetted your appetite and you want to know more, you can learn in depth through the study book *Astrological Psychology: The Huber Method*, edited by Barry Hopewell. This book is essentially the course material of the English-language distance learning courses that were offered for many years by the Astrological Psychology Association in the UK. A wealth of further resources, including books, software for generating charts, tutors and consultants are referenced from the website www.astrologicalpsychology.org.

One of the aims of the Astrological Psychology Association and the above website has been to promote and develop the concept of astrological psychology amongst astrologers, psychologists, counsellors and others engaged in the helping professions, as well as making it available to all interested in self-understanding and self-development, and in the evolution of humanity.

It is important that practitioners of astrological psychology adopt an ethical approach, so that they knowingly do no harm to their clients and work always from the highest motives. The Hubers promoted a suitable code of ethics which has been adopted by all astrological psychology practitioners.

Astrological psychology is based on an understanding of the human being as a whole person who is connected to the environment and the material world but who is also a spiritual being able to take responsibility for him or herself. The responsibility lies with each and every one of us to be this spiritual being in the best way we possibly can. Astrological psychology gives us a path leading in this direction.

Summary – Bringing It All Together

- Chart interpretation involves a combination of understanding of technical features in the chart and intuitive response to the chart. A checklist is given for the main features to look for in the chart.

- This needs to be combined with wide experience of working with the charts of real people and gaining their personal feedback.

- Two examples are provided of the interpretation of the charts of real people, together with their feedback.

- This book has only provided an introduction. Further study, and much practical experience, are necessary before you can effectively practise counselling using astrological psychology.

- The book *Astrological Psychology: The Huber Method*, based on the Diploma course previously offered by the Astrological Psychology Association, covers the full richness of techniques outlined in this book, plus more advanced techniques.

- To practise astrological counselling, it is also necessary to have appropriate training in counselling, and to consider whether to also train in basic psychosynthesis.

- Resources to support your further study of astrological psychology can be found at the website www.astrologicalpsychology.org..

Bibliography

2 Astrological Psychology in Context

Historical Context

The Great Year, Nicholas Campion (Historical perspective)
Astrology and the Seven Rays, Bruno & Louise Huber, (Sumerians)
Fears, Phobias and Panic, Wolfhard König, published by APA (Asklepius)
Passion of the Western Mind, Richard Tarnas (Development of Western ideas)
The Last Hours of Ancient Sunlight, Thom Hartmann (Global crisis)

Psychology and Spirituality

Memories, Dreams and Reflections, C.G.Jung (Autobiography)
Psychosynthesis, Roberto Assagioli (Psychosynthesis)
The World's Religions, Huston Smith (Religions)
The Secret Doctrine, H.P.Blavatsky (New spiritual approaches)
The Light of the Soul, Alice Bailey (Eastern influence)

Changing paradigm

A Theory of Everything, Ken Wilber (Integral world view)
Living in Connection, Chris Clarke (New science)
The Marriage of Sense and Soul, Ken Wilber (Science and subjectivity)
Radical Nature, Christian de Quincey (Nature of consciousness)

Development of astrological psychology

Esoteric Psychology I and II, Alice Bailey (Spiritual roots)
Esoteric Astrology, Alice Bailey (Spiritual roots)
The Astrology of Personality, Dane Rudhyar (Psychological astrology)
Astrological Psychosynthesis, Bruno and Louise Huber (Huber Method)

3 The Five Levels of Human Existence

The Astrological Houses, Bruno and Louise Huber

4 Looking at the Whole Chart

Astrological Psychosynthesis, Bruno and Louise Huber

5 Aspect Patterns

Aspect Pattern Astrology, Bruno, Louise, Michael Huber
Aspect Patterns in Colour, Joyce Hopewell

6 The Planets and Psychological Drives

The Planets and their Psychological Meaning, Bruno and Louise Huber
Astrological Psychosynthesis, Bruno and Louise Huber

7 The Signs
Church Monastery Cathedral, Herbert Whone (Church symbolism)
Reflections and Meditations on the Signs of the Zodiac, Louise Huber

8 The Houses and the Environment
The Astrological Houses, Bruno and Louise Huber

9 Nature versus Nurture
Astrological Psychosynthesis, Bruno and Louise Huber (Family Model)

10 Life Clock
Life Clock, Bruno and Louise Huber
Using Age Progression, by Joyce Hopewell

11 Psychological and Spiritual Development
Reflections and Meditations on the Signs of the Zodiac, Louise Huber
The Way of Passion: A Celebration of Rumi, Andrew Harvey (Stages 1-4)
Psychosynthesis: The Elements and Beyond, Will Parfitt (Assagioli and Quabala)
Fears, Phobias and Panic, Wolfhard Konig, published by APA (Fear)
Astrological Psychosynthesis, Bruno and Louise Huber (Personality integration)
Transformation: Astrology as a Spiritual Path, Bruno and Louise Huber (Life Clock)
Moon Node Astrology, Bruno and Louise Huber (Moon Nodes)

12 Bringing It All Together

Sample interpretations
The Living Birth Chart, by Joyce Hopewell
Astrological Psychosynthesis, Bruno and Louise Huber
LifeClock, Bruno and Louise Huber
The website www.astrologicalpsychology.org also contains a number of chart interpretations.